Aquinas and King

Aquinas and King

A Discourse on Civil Disobedience

Charles P. Nemeth

Chair and Professor of Graduate Legal Studies
California University of Pennsylvania

Carolina Academic Press
Durham, North Carolina

Library of Congress Cataloging-in-Publication Data

Nemeth, Charles P., 1951-
  Aquinas and King : a discourse on civil disobedience / Charles P.
Nemeth. -- 1st.
      p. cm.
  Includes bibliographical references.
  ISBN 978-1-59460-638-0 (alk. paper)
  1. Civil disobedience. 2. Thomism. 3. Thomas, Aquinas, Saint,
1225?-1274. 4. King, Martin Luther, Jr., 1929-1968 I. Title.

  K3269.N46 2008
  342.08'54--dc22

                                              2008049676

CAROLINA ACADEMIC PRESS
700 Kent Street
Durham, North Carolina 27701
Telephone (919) 489-7486
Fax (919) 493-5668
www.cap-press.com

Dedication

To Michael Augustine Nemeth—youngest son,
of good heart and an intellect soon to unfold.

To St. Thomas Aquinas, who states:

Man is subject to God absolutely in all respects both
within and without, and therefore he is bound to obey
Him in all things. But inferiors are subject to their superiors, not in all things, but in certain matters of limited
range; and in those matters superiors are intermediaries
between God and their subjects: in other matters the latter are subject immediately to God, by whom they are in-
structed through the natural or the written law.

(Summa Theologica, II-II, Question CIV)

Contents

Preface

Those familiar with the works of St. Thomas Aquinas are forever amazed at the prophetic relevance of the Angelic Doctor. By prophetic, we mean that he seems to understand not only causes and effects but the proper remedies for any temporal injustice. By this I mean, that St. Thomas has an answer for just about everything. And when the stakes are at their highest, his answers always seem to make the most sense.

Civil Disobedience is one such problem. During the tumult of the 1960s, the American character was tested in extraordinary ways —none more pressing than the rightful clamor for civil rights in the Black community. Existing laws institutionalized the second class citizenry in many quarters and courts were very unsympathetic to the obvious injustices coursing through the American experience. Laws were plentiful—most of which served to maintain the unjust status quo. Those seeking reform had a variety of options open when challenging these wrongs. That the challenge was justified is undeniable. The method of challenge could include violent revolution, passive resistance, legislative lobbying and public protest to name just a few. For St. Thomas, unjust laws not only did not bind or oblige the citizen; these enactments could not be simply disregarded in hope for better days. St. Thomas urges the citizen to resist and undermine injustice for unjust human laws cannot "bind a man in conscience, and if it conflicts with a higher law, human law should not be obeyed."[1]

Consider the life and times of Martin Luther King, Jr. How did Dr. King arrive at a philosophy of nonviolent civil disobedience to the inequalities of his day? Why did he choose this method of structural challenge over the other options? Dr. King could have gone in very different directions. For example, he could have adopted the militant stance of the Black Panther, or in the alternative he could have sided with those calling for complete, open and violent rebellion. Or he could have urged his followers to separate from white society since some movements held that any alliance with the former "master" was not only distasteful but also completely unproductive. That King had alternatives is a fact often forgotten. So the seminal question becomes, why did Dr. King advocate a resistance rooted in complete nonviolence? Why did he passionately urge his followers to lay down the sword, to accept suffering and humiliation rather than strike his errant and hateful neighbor, and to willingly and very humbly experience the jail cell for his alleged crimes? King passionately argues:

> I've seen too much hate to want to hate, myself, and I've seen hate on the faces of too many sheriffs, too many white citizens' councilors, and too many Klansmen of the South to want to hate, myself; and every time I see it, I say to myself, hate is too great a burden to bear. Somehow we must be able to stand up before our most bitter opponents and say: We shall match your capacity to inflict suffering by our capacity to endure suffering. We will meet your physical force with soul force. Do to us what you will and we will still love you. We cannot in all good conscience obey your unjust laws and abide by an unjust system, because non-cooperation with evil is as much a moral obligation as cooperation with good, and so throw us in jail and we will still love you.[2]

It is King that fully understands that "the dignity of the human person flows from the fact that the human person is created in the image of God, redeemed by Jesus Christ, and thereby promised eternal life with God."[3]

I think when one examines the man, his life and his work, both written and oratorical, only one conclusion is possible—that Dr. Martin Luther King, Jr. was in fact a Thomist through and through. Not a Thomist on all things, but as to his understanding of law and its corresponding obligation or lack thereof, King is the ultimate Thomist. In his letters and writings, texts and speeches, Dr. King is a regular advocate of the philosophy of St. Thomas Aquinas. You can feel the respect that King has for Thomist principles, and in a sense, Thomism is the "antidote" against the ravages of modernity.[4] King's theory of civil disobedience classically adheres to the teachings of St. Thomas Aquinas. Amazingly, he even tells us about his allegiance to the philosophy of St. Thomas. That is what this humble work is all about—a discourse and discernment into the compatibility of both men and a revelation that once again, St. Thomas had the answers long before the problem ever emerged.

In *Chapter 1*, the reader is introduced to rudiments of law—what is means; how it is defined; whether human law depends upon a higher law or rests sufficiently in its own promulgation, or whether law is tied to a morality. Any theory of civil disobedience needs this foundational understanding. Considerable attention is given to the legal theory of St. Thomas since King will come to depend upon it in his rationalization for civil disobedience. Hence, the chapter examines the types of law, eternal, natural, divine and human, as well as how these types of law are interlocked and unified. The role of the natural law on human legal reasoning is stressed. Justification for civil disobedience will depend upon the higher law jurisprudence espoused by both King and Aquinas.

Chapter 2 defines civil disobedience and lays out the necessary parameters for justified disobedience to an existing law. First, the advocate of civil disobedience must demonstrate the injustice of a given law. How does one distinguish the just from the unjust law? Second, how does a human law undergo this sort of moral scrutiny? What standards or measures will find that a particular human law is just? Does the law in question uplift or denigrate the human person and does the law assure the appropriate distribution of wealth, honors and economic opportunity? Third, what method of civil disobedience is consistent with proper moral action? Is non-violence a mandatory method of resistance or can the party advocating civil disobedience do so violently? For Aquinas and King, the only acceptable method of resistance will be non-violent in design. Fourth, is the advocate willing to protest and resist in an open, visible setting as if the whole world need know of the action's intent and purpose? Moral, civil disobedience seeks to educate the collective and bring about change in an open setting. Finally, particularly in the case of Dr. King, the role of suffering receives significant attention. Suffering rests firmly in the ethos of civil disobedience. Suffering is a predictable effect for those engaged in public resistance. As Christ suffered on the cross for the sins and errors of humanity, so too the resistor, who witnesses injustice and stands firm against it, fully expects to suffer a wide array of consequences.

At *Chapter 3*, the stress includes the relationship of civil disobedience with the duty and obligations of the Christian moral agent. Being a Christian prompts Christian responsibility in human affairs. Claiming Christianity assumes a certain righteousness in human conduct while expecting resistance to those things in opposition to the moral truths discoverable in Christianity. For both King and Aquinas, the relationship of faith and reason is fully developed and not severable. In each, the centrality of Jesus Christ in the affairs of the world is not in doubt, nor is the role of love and charity when dealing with those who heap injustice upon us. For King and Aquinas, it is the truth of Christ and his philosophy that drives the enterprise and it is the commandment, to love one's neighbor as I have loved you, that shapes the form and methodology of resistance. Civil disobedience lacks legitimacy unless rooted in the divine, the higher jurisprudence of an all powerful and loving God. Civil disobedience leaps beyond the simple affairs unraveling on the streets but finds its anchor in the perfection of the Creative God. In the world of Aquinas and King, non-violence in the display of civil disobedience is fully compatible with the Christian life. Violence assaults the Christian ethic since it is an "immoral means to attain moral ends."[5]

In *Chapter 4* we discover the "radical" jurisprudence of St. Thomas and Martin Luther King. In the view of St. Thomas, the moral agent refuses to recognize the existence of a particular promulgation. The refusal to recognize is grounded in the inherent injustice of the law in question. Here the moral player rejects not only the content of the law but also refuses the label or designation "law" applied to its content. To refuse recognition implies a complete resistance to the content of the law as well as its formula alleging to be a law. St. Thomas will term these unjust enactments as not law but "acts of violence rather than laws."[6] Such laws cannot bind in conscience and cannot require compliance on the part of the resistor. For Dr. King a similar conclusion will be reached. King will query whether the human law "squares with the moral order" and whether a law in opposition to the law of God can bind in any sense. King concludes that,

> God walks with us. He has placed within the very structure of this universe certain absolute moral laws. We can neither defy nor break them. If we disobey them, they will break us.[7]

Chapter 5 concludes that the respective philosophies Dr. Martin Luther King, Jr., and St. Thomas Aquinas are fundamentally compatible. When King explicitly mentions St. Thomas in his *Letter from the Birmingham Jail,* we can only conclude that King's theory depends upon a traditional theological and philosophical outlook. King could not be plainer when he remarks,

> A just law is a manmade code that squares with the moral law or the law of God. An unjust law is a code that is out of harmony with the moral law. To put it in the terms of St. Thomas Aquinas: An unjust law is a human law that is not rooted in the eternal or natural law.[8]

King's entire theory of civil disobedience depends upon a "metaphysical otherness" or a "transphysics" that forces the human actor to look beyond the positive law. The legitimacy of the cause will tie directly to the perfection of the higher order he advocates. Equality does not arise strictly from the legislative process but finds a home in the dignity of the man, the worth and value of all free and rational beings created in the image of God. Rights are teth-

ered to a perfect God who authors all human existence. These
rights are permanent and universal and not subject to the whims
of men. As a result, both King and Aquinas chart a path of civil
disobedience that will blend faith and reason, human law and divine law, as well as a form of non-violent disobedience that will
resist injustice. For all things "created by God, whether it be contingent or necessary, is subject to the eternal law."[9]

In the final analysis, each thinker looks to the heavens when
shaping a theory of civil disobedience. It is an incredible story—
that a 20th century Civil Rights leader, arguably this nation's greatest proponent of non-violent civil disobedience, derived his wisdom from the genius of St. Thomas—a scholar whose ideas have
never been more relevant.

Charles P. Nemeth, J.D., Ph.D., LL.M.
Pittsburgh, Pennsylvania
March 2009

Acknowledgments

This is the third text I have humbly crafted regarding the mind of St. Thomas Aquinas. Never can I forget those that help me along the way. First, my staff at California University, namely Laurel Manderino, Administrative Assistant Extraordinaire, and Rose Mahouski, keeper of the mail and everything else, free this writer from the many tasks that sometimes interfere with creative exposition. My thanks are perpetual. Gratitude is keenly felt for our university President, Dr. Angelo Armenti and my Dean, Dr. Len Colelli—both of whom support these endeavors and understand their importance.

Thanks to Carolina Academic Press for tackling this important analysis. In an age when things previous to modernity are looked at askew, Carolina is a welcome home for this production. To the publisher, Keith Sipe, I extend my appreciation as well as to Karen Clayton in production.

As always, I am glad to have Hope Haywood look at the final product. Few people have the penchant for detail she has. It is a remarkable skill that I cherish.

Finally, my love and affection for my friend and partner for 38 years, Jean Marie, and the 7 children we have been blessed to receive, is forever extended.

Charles P. Nemeth, J.D., Ph.D., LL.M.
Pittsburgh, Pennsylvania
March 2009

Aquinas and King

CHAPTER 1

The Concept of Law in Aquinas and King

Introduction

Any defensible theory of civil disobedience demands a look at first principles. Aside from definitional questions, the advocate of civil disobedience initially evaluates the justice or injustice in a particular law. Before that the moral agent needs to understand the nature of law itself since the law provides the rationale for the objection. Hence, one asks what is law in the eyes of St. Thomas and Martin Luther King, Jr.? Are their visions of law consistent or compatible with contemporary definitions? Or did both these thinkers rely on another form of jurisprudence to erect their theory of civil disobedience?

In the worlds of King and Aquinas we discern a full recognition that human law can only go so far, and in the final analysis, the problems of injustice and inhumanity are fundamentally resolved by "a willingness of men to obey the unenforceable."[1] How men justify racism and inequality cannot be described as noble. At times the legal landscape that King encountered was utterly distressing and marked "by a temptation to despair because it is clear now how deep and systematic are the evils it confronts."[2] Human laws are what subjected him to a myriad of indignities. Human laws promoting and enforcing segregation, King argues, "have caused the darkness...."[3] Human law provides both remedy and curse in the world of Dr. King but before he employs the promulgations of man, he will adhere to a Thomistic vision of law. It is his anchor in a sea of social turbulence.

Both men will define law in ways we are historically comfortable with and in ways that rattle our cages. Questions regarding definition and scope, the interplay between law and morality, the role of Theology, Scripture and the Gospel of Jesus Christ in legal reasoning, as well as the basic definitional qualities of the law are fully assessed. Exactly how these jurisprudential conclusions shape their respective theories of civil disobedience is the chief aim of this chapter.

The Nature of Law According to St. Thomas Aquinas

Most contemporary schools of jurisprudence tie the law's definition to its enactment or promulgation. The power of law depends upon case or statute, rule or regulation. Law, in brief, consists of the words that emerge from the legislative or regulatory process. Positivism, which holds that laws derive their force and power from promulgation, is the predominant contemporary jurisprudence.[4]

This approach is woefully inadequate in the world of St. Thomas. In contrast, his vision is properly described as "eudemonistic and teleological" and "Natural."[5] Human law is "designed to help men lead the best possible lives."[6] Law may take the form of enactment or code, and come into existence by promulgation and other legislative process, but this characterization dwells upon a singular facet of Thomas' jurisprudence. St. Thomas would hold that positivism is a jurisprudence of futility, "fighting a losing battle."[7] Aquinas respects promulgation, but only to a point. For Aquinas gazes at higher orders—the natural, the divine and the eternal. When human laws are inconsistent with these higher orders he will even encourage two things: first, *non-recognition*—a view that holds that the so called "law" is not a law at all; and secondly, *non-observance*—a requirement that one refuse its power, that the citizen affirmatively not observe it requirements. When human laws are contrary to the natural, divine and eternal laws, he labels them "unjust" and deserving no allegiance or compliance. In contrast to positivism, unjust laws have no power, force or effect. Unjust laws do not bind in conscience, says St. Thomas.

> On the other hand, laws may be unjust in two ways: first, by being contrary to the human good, through being op-

posed to the things mentioned above—either in respect
to the end ... or in respect of the author, as when a man
makes a law that goes beyond the power committed to
him ... [8]

Hence when laws are contrary or inconsistent to the natural law
or the eternal law of God, these are "acts of violence rather than
laws." Such laws "do not bind in conscience"[9] and according to
Aquinas, unjust laws are not laws at all.[10] Thomas' just law theory
is a compelling and prophetic analysis of the human person's rights
and obligations before the law, and further evidence of the law's
derivative quality. Considered from various fronts, it is an account
that deals with the justice, the equity of a law itself, the enforceability or obligatoriness of an unjust or just law, and the right to
disobey its content. Thomas queries whether every law "binds"[11]
men in conscience. If justly enacted, the answer is affirmative, since
justice is consistent with reason and the perfect justice of God. Man
is *not* bound to obey any unjust law because it lacks the force and
nature of a law. In both contexts, the law's legitimacy is derived
from a higher order. A law is just if "ordained to the common
good,"[12] the divine good[13] and nature itself. Thomas advises direct
disobedience to any law "contrary to the commandments of God"[14]
since such laws are "beyond the scope of human power."[15] For laws
in contravention to these principles, the human actor is not obliged
or bound; neither can the state legitimately impress such laws upon
its citizenry. Scholars have debated vigorously whether St. Thomas
holds to the Augustinian maxim that *an unjust law is not a law at
all* (*lex injusta non est lex*). Thomas exhibits more caution in this
language: "That which is not just seems to be no law at all."[16]

At *Question 96, Article 4*, in his *Summa Theologica*, St. Thomas
summarizes how a law can be unjust "(1) if it is not directed to the
common good; (2) if it is beyond the authority of the law-giver;
and (3) if it does not impose properly proportionate burdens."[17]
In any of these cases, the law loses its force as law and cannot
oblige its target. Any disregard for the eternal or natural law principles enunciated above is surely evidence of injustice. Laws crafted
in derogation to the common good, an anarchy of competing,

non-aligned interests replacing a common bond with "as many rules or measures as there are things measured or ruled, ... cease to be of use."[18]

For Thomas, there is a "law that is beyond the law" which guides human operations. Igor Grazin labels this law the "Imperatives of the Highest Nature" given "us by the mercy and wisdom of the truly Supreme Legislator."[19] This law, consisting of first principles, secondary deductions and prudential insights—impressions of the Creator that shapes our essence, which is burned and impressed into our very fiber—is just as much part of our humanity and legal infrastructure as the codification. Noel McDermott remarks:

> There is a sense, in which the law is inhuman, but the law beyond the law is entirely human, and the judge who takes account of it is simply thinking in human terms as well as legal terms.... The law beyond the law is simply the law of his own humanness, an intuition of the human in himself which demands great lucidity and humility.[20]

All law maintains its connection to this law above the law and "retain{s} a certain universality" and "impose{s} some rational pattern on an otherwise chaotic element" known as the collective.[21] Compellingly, St. Thomas argues that human beings need law as a form of habituation and training, and without the regularizing influences, the bulk of the populace would descend into the strictly pleasurable. In his *Commentary on Aristotle's Nicomachean Ethics*, he poses this extraordinary ideal for a law:

> But it is difficult; he shows that legislation is required for virtuous habituation. First, he shows that all men become virtuous by means of law. Next ... he shows that this cannot be done properly without law.... And that it is difficult for anyone to be guided from his youth to virtue according to good customs unless he is reared under excellent laws by which a kind of necessity impels a man to good.[22]

In this sense, law is necessary for the masses on two fronts: first, for the already good to give support and sustenance to their goodness; and secondly, to those who operate only out of consequence or fear.

Characteristics of Law According to Aquinas

A common conception of law is that of a rule, regulation, statute or ordinance, a case issued by judicial authority, or some other concretization of a particular legal idea or principle. *Laws* are as numerous and meaningful as the scope of their coverage, and are, without much argument, *juridical* instruments. By *juridical* the law's content commands, prohibits, enhances, advances or restricts a good or end. As comprehended by St. Thomas, law is juridical,[23] but only partially. Thomas paints the broadest picture of law possible. First, law is synonymous with God, with rationality, and a rational plan of creation and operations. Even the irrational creature, as directed by God through natural inclination, has a legalistic quality. Law pertains to the species. St. Thomas describes:

> Just as the acts of irrational creatures are directed by God through a rational plan which pertains to their species, so are the acts of men directed by God inasmuch as they pertain to the individual, as we have shown. But the acts of irrational creatures, as pertaining to the species, are directed by God through natural inclination, which goes along with the nature of the species. Therefore, over and above this, something must be given to men whereby they may be directed in their own personal acts. And this we call law.[24]

Therefore, Thomistic law defines itself in a more profound sense beyond promulgation, for the law's essence mirrors the fullness of God's creation, the nature of his creatures and the unfolding of species and their corresponding operations. Some have argued that St. Thomas' perspective on law is almost cosmic—a reflection of how all movement occurs, whether that of the heavenly body, the animal or plant, or the laws of physics. Anton-Hermann Chroust discovers a *universal cosmic orderliness* in Thomistic jurisprudence:

First, the ontological order in which being as such tends towards the preservation of its own being in accordance with its ontological nature. In the case of man this inclination manifests itself in the preservation of life and in all of man's actions conducive to this preservation. Secondly, the vitalistic order in which being tends towards positive action. In the case of man this tendency becomes an inclination to act appropriately and in accordance with his own being and purpose. And, thirdly, the order of the rational and social animal which is also the domain of free, moral self-determination.[25]

In a way, each of Chroust's assertions is valid because St. Thomas perceives law as an ordination, an impetus, an activity seeking proper ends, a fulfillment of essence and perfection of operation. Etienne Gilson eloquently corroborates:

The first, and the vastest of all, is the universe. All beings created by God and maintained in existence by His will, can be regarded as one huge society in which all of us are members, along with animals, and even with things. There is not a single creature, animate or inanimate, which does not act in conformity with certain ends. Animals and things are subject to these rules and tend toward their ends without knowing them. Man, on the contrary, is conscious of them, and his moral justice consists in accepting them voluntarily. All the laws of nature, all the laws of morality or of society ought to be considered as so many particular cases of one single law, divine law. Now, God's rule for the government of the universe is, like God Himself, necessarily eternal. Thus the name *eternal law* is given to this first law, sole source of all others.[26]

Law is supreme, divine legislation in addition to its positive codification or ordinance; it is the plan for a life consistent with this divine rationality—a life of virtue, and it is the order "whereby man clings to God."[27]

Law as the "Rule and Measure" of Reason

In Thomas' view, law is a "certain rational plan and rule of operation"[28] and especially proper "to rational creatures only."[29] St. Thomas confidently asserts that "law is something pertaining to reason"[30] and a measure of human activity. If it is a measure of human action, one must presuppose there is a connection to human reason, since only the human species analyzes, deliberates, and counsels about activity and movement. St. Thomas asserts that law is a rational exercise:

> Since law is a kind of rule and measure, it may be in something in two ways. First, as in that which measures and rules and since this is proper to reason, it follows that, in this way, law is in the reason alone. Secondly, as in that which is ruled and measured. In this way, law is in all those things that are inclined to something by reason of some law, so that any inclination arising from a law may be called a law.[31]

Stated concisely, the law represents rationality and orderliness in individual and rational existence. Law, aside from its enactment, is the handmaiden of reason itself. When dealing with the law's essence, St. Thomas imparts primary stature to reason:

> Law is a rule and measure of acts, whereby man is induced to act or is restrained from acting; for *lex* [law] is derived from *ligare* [to bind], because it binds one to act. Now the rule and measure of human acts is the reason, which is the first principle of human acts, as is evident from what has been stated above. For it belongs to the reason to direct to the end, which is the first principle in all matters of action, according to the Philosopher.[32]

Law as an Instrument of the Common Good

St. Thomas is well aware that the ordinating influence of law does not terminate with individual activity, because it just as pertinently applies to the common good of a nation as it applies to the common good of its individual citizenry. In response to whether a law should be crafted for the individual or common case, St. Thomas indicates that every human law derives legitimacy from its relationship to the common interest. Laws consist of far more than individual applications but are germane to the life of a nation. "Hence human laws should be proportioned to the common good. Now the common good comprises many things. Therefore law should take account of many things, as to persons, as to matters, and as to times."[33]

With keen insight, Thomas discerns the futility of a law that applies in the individual scenario alone. Laws are implemented not for the single person or the one-time circumstance, but instead law is a common precept applicable to a community of men.[34] It is for the multitude that laws exist, because laws for the community are nothing more than the social sum of its members. Law, particularly the human variety, "is framed for the multitude of beings."[35] Law is equated with the happiness in both individual and culture. If lacking a communal component, the enactment would be "devoid of the nature of law."[36]

Law as Good and End

The concept of the *good*, rests heavily in Thomistic jurisprudence, whether temporal, temporary ones, or the ultimate good, the penultimate end of man—God, holistic in style, universal in approach. Thomistic law pulls in all that is good, beautiful, and perfect and finds final solace only in the beatific vision. Thomistic jurisprudence embraces more than the functionality of utilitarianism, the artificiality of Marxism[37], and transformative humanism. A theory of law, so says St. Thomas, is loftier, rising above "prejudice and passion[38]," and fixing "upon eternal reasons to reaffirm a forgotten truth, formulate a new principle, or overturn an established error."[39]

To be consistent with reason, man seeks perfection in every category of life. He or she can will otherwise, but in the intricate and incomprehensible act of creation itself, God could not fashion a being who would command his or her own destruction. Since the Creator is all-good, so too the creatures molded in his image. These ideas will be more easily understood in the context of Aquinas' various kinds of law, specifically the *eternal, natural, divine* and *human*. Man's reason, the artifice of law itself, can readily discover these ends. Perfect, unreserved happiness resides only in the splendor of divine perfection. "Perfect orderliness,"[40] as Chroust terms it, is "declaratory of the *summum bonum*, that is, of God."[41]

At every level of Thomistic thinking, legal or otherwise, God is the ultimate end of the reasoning, intellectual creature. St. Thomas urges us, "Now, from what has been seen earlier, it is established that God is the ultimate end of the whole of things; that an intellectual nature alone attains to Him in Himself, that is by knowing and loving Him, as is evident from what has been said."[42]

The Various Kinds of Law

To fathom Thomistic jurisprudence correctly, teleologically, one must engage the concept of "law." Positivism, the idea that laws are laws because of promulgation will not do. St. Thomas, impressed with the power of human law, though aware of its limitations, designs a multi-tiered construct, a hierarchical architectonic of laws in four categories: the *eternal*, the *natural*, the *divine* and the *human*. These four types exist independently, yet dependently: they are distinct, yet unified and integrated. Succinctly put, the hierarchy implies unity, but is dedicated to a priority of one type of law over the others. An elementary depiction would be as shown.

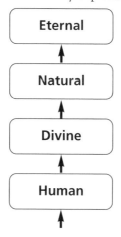

In the plan of God, the higher law descends to the lower law. Thomas sees lower forms of the law as *derived* from the higher form. This "derivative"[43] quality commences with the eternal law, the Divine exemplar which is the blueprint for the universe and its law. Divine revelation, centrally exposed in biblical instruction, gives clarification to the people of God. Creation, especially the rational variety, participates in the eternal law by and through the natural law. Positive laws, the promulgations of man, are a necessary component for a civil society. Unified and interdependent in design, Thomistic law is complicated yet elementary. At its peak, God's eternal law watches over the other categories. "The exemplar of divine Wisdom is the eternal law,"[44] Thomas relates, and as a result "all laws proceed from the eternal law."[45]

At the human level, each derives its legitimacy from its superior counterpart. A Judge, jurist, lawmaker and lawyer cannot differentiate or chop-up their legal inquiry, *e.g.*, forgetting man's natural inclination in a case of sodomy; proclaiming a humanistic notion of individual rights at the expense of common welfare; enacting a statute, interpreting a case, applying a principle, without regard for spiritual, moral or revelatory considerations. Pure functionalism, legal emotivism or subjectivism, lack the larger framework advanced by St. Thomas. Within the *Treatise on Law*, St. Thomas offers a series of interlocking and interdependent categories of law—each form gauged in its relationship to the others before legal action will have legitimacy. The clamor of the crowd and weeping and gnashing of the individual will not suffice.

The Eternal Law

At the pinnacle in Thomistic jurisprudence is the *eternal* law of God, the rational architect of the universe and its creatures. God, as author and architect, expresses perfection, omniscience and pure thought. God, by and through His *eternal law*, fashions an exemplar for man and His universe. The *eternal law*, as Gilson urges, is that which "makes us what we are."[46] The *lex aeterna* is the blueprint for an ordered existence, the benchmark for perfection in every facet of existence. It is "the objective and absolute *a priori* of everything that may properly be called a rule and a measure."[47]

In calling God's law the "supreme exemplar,"[48] Aquinas foundationally sets the basis for all legal practice and theory in this perennial, permanent and immutable dimension. God, the artist and the craftsman, makes only good things, and as a result, molds creatures with lawful inclinations and components. Aquinas characterizes objects or beings by the "emanation"[49] from God's being, containing or being the law itself and the "extensiveness" of God's influence on reality itself. The perfection of God is not an unbridgeable valley, due to God's creative relationship with His authorship of the world. Creation possesses an artistic or demonstrative quality that inevitably and intimately bonds Creator with the created. The Divine God moves "all things to their due end,"[50] and "bears the character of law."[51]

The perfect God naturally has a perfect legal constitution, though His complete content and subject matter are unknowable to temporal species like man. The *eternal law* is incapable of promulgation since such promulgation is *a priori* and self-evident.[52] Thomas recognizes the human inadequacy of knowing directly and primarily what the eternal actually is—since the law is God Himself. What is irrefutable, is only God knows His own eternal law in its fullness. As imperfect beings, we can struggle only to know the effects of the eternal law. Thomas holds that we "cannot know the things that are of God as they are in themselves; but they are made known to us in their effects, according to *Rom. i. 20: The invisible things of God … are clearly seen, being understood by the things that are made.*"[53]

St. Thomas is wise enough to equate the eternal law of God with that of God Himself. All that is created by God, "whether contingent or necessary, is subject to the eternal law."[54] God's law is the supreme norm for all living beings and creation. Governance of the universe by God imputes a law of operations. Thomas simultaneously uses the term "government" when God is described as "the ruler of the universe"[55]. This rule has the quality of and the "nature of a law."[56]

When St. Thomas queries whether all human affairs are subject to the eternal law, only an answer in the affirmative is possible. Even the wicked and the perverse are subject to the eternal law. Even the "blessed and the damned are under the eternal law."[57] Even the ignorant cannot disavow some knowledge of the eternal law since their being still reflects the Creator by its effects. Even the lustful and the slaves of flesh cannot "dominate"[58] and destroy the good of one's nature, for "there remains in man the inclination to do the things which belong to the eternal law."[59] Nothing and no one can evade the eternal law. The eternal law, residing within, or more accurately inherently within, the God of Creation, is the measure of all activity. Thomas does not hesitate calling God's law *truth* itself. At *Question 93, Article 1*, in the *Summa Theologica,* he summarizes that "the divine intellect is true in itself, and its exemplar is truth itself."[60]

St. Thomas' evaluation of law cannot and does not end here; practical and pragmatic reality would not allow it. As creatures, as living agents of God's creation, and simultaneously recognizing our own inadequacies to comprehend the eternal law, we need a legal benchmark that can be understood—the *natural law.*

The Natural Law

Since the human species is powerless to fully learn the mind of God and His eternal law, St. Thomas recommends a look at our very natures. Nature, in a scientific, physical sense has an order, a series of operational rules. Nature "in its purity ... is rather like the word life."[61] Man is a creature of nature and thereby subsists of rules and operational qualities. C.S. Lewis' critical mind poses the foundational meaning of nature. "By far the commonest native meaning of *natura* is something like sort, kind, quality, or character. When you ask, in our modern idiom, what something 'is like', you are asking for its *natura*. When you want to tell a man the *natura* of anything you describe the thing."[62] Thomas gets to the core of nature in his work, *On Kingship,* for "whatever is in accord with nature is best, for in all things nature does what is best."[63]

As author of nature, God could not and would not forge a creation of disorder and anarchy, but more predictably, infuses and imprints an orderly, lawful, natural sequence in each of His creatures. "The manifold and beautiful order of nature is the work of a designing mind of vast intelligence; and must be ultimately explained by the existence of a personal God."[64] Undoubtedly, human beings like other beings, display natural inclinations, preferences, propensities and dispositions that mirror the wisdom of the author. Gilson artfully offers this analysis: "Granted this, it is clear that the precepts of natural law correspond exactly with our natural inclinations and that their order is the same. Man is, to begin with, a being like all others. More particularly, he is a living being, like all other animals. Finally, by the privilege of this nature, he is a rational being. Thus it is that three great natural laws bind him, each in its' own way."[65] The term, *natural law*, references two critical Thomistic ideas: 1) the nature of a being itself; and, 2) law as an operation of that nature. To say someone or something has a nature is to typify its very existence. Then, apply law to that nature and that nature unfolds before us—doing what it must and should do to preserve its existence, signifies nature as well.[66] Nor is the natural law some changeable phenomena deposited in the creature for the moment. St. Thomas resists the effort to call the natural law an habituation because habits increase or decrease while natures are fixed.[67] Habits increase, decrease, tends toward good things or malevolent ones. Natures are poured during a being's construction phase. A loose and impressive comparison might be this: as the eternal law is God Himself, the natural law is a mirror of really what we are as beings, because this is the eternal plan. The natural law is imprinted on man, infused into his or her nature, "written" in their hearts. How could it be otherwise when the creature reflects the Maker? Regularly found within the body of St. Thomas' work, is the term "imprint" which represents the mark of the maker. The human person partakes and participates in the eternal law of God. Human beings "derive their respective inclinations to their proper acts and ends."[68] Rational creatures among all others participate most generally, Thomas remarks; "the rational creature is subject to divine providence in a more excellent way, in so far as it itself partakes of a share of providence, by being provident both for itself and for others. Therefore it has a share of the eternal reason, whereby it has a natural inclination to its proper act and end; and this participation of the eternal law in the rational creature is called the natural law."[69]

One should not think that St. Thomas' natural law to be solely biological—it is much more comprehensive, more ambitious. A biological phenomenon would act out of necessity or pure function while Thomas' natural being moves primarily due to its rational form. Thomistic natural law fully expects reason to be the receiver of God's design. Nor is it a series of legal annotations, codifications and enactments. More aptly, the natural law is a reflection of the whole, or, as Ignatius Eschmann cogently defines the Natural Law, as "not a statute enacted by the divine Legislator, but is the self-same act by which the Creator brought into being our rational nature."[70] Inclinations, tendencies and propensities are not blank, intellectual exercises, especially since the natural law theory of St. Thomas centrally depends upon *reason* for its discernment. Natural law for St. Thomas is more than Newtonian physics or evolutionary development. Natural law for St. Thomas, is in service to the human condition, and is easily gleaned from human operation.

That water travels to its lowest point, or that bears propagate their species is not natural law activity as St. Thomas defines it. "It is nature itself that is, more precisely, rational nature; it is reason understood as the power of reasoning."[71] Only rational creatures possess the natural law. Natural law is about inclinations and imprints—how the human creature lives in accordance with their overall constitution. The human player living compatibly with these natural impressions, lives as the Creator intended. Natural law cannot be removed, "blotted out,"[72] moreover, it cannot be forgotten nor can its content be denied on the basis of ignorance. Natural law is the human person's *participation* in the eternal law of God. "Thus man has a natural inclination to know the truth about God, and to live in society; and in this respect, whatever pertains to this inclination belongs to the natural law: *e.g.*, to shun ignorance, to avoid offending those among whom one has to live, and other such things regarding the above inclination."[73]

From the Thomistic view, man is forged so tightly with the natural law that he cannot extricate himself from its influence. We can't even intend contrary to what we are, though we can *will* the difference—choosing evil which "is a result apart from intention."[74] Wickedness, unlawfulness, does not reside in reason or our constitution, for "such a thing is not the necessary result of what is intended; rather, it is repugnant to what is intended."[75] St. Thomas does not compartmentalize the natural law's influence on human operations but recognizes its determinative power. Every inclination in the human actor, particularly those touched or controlled by reason, deals with our natural law imprint.[76]

Those who argue its relativity, inapplicability, and selectivity as to person or precept, would be at odds with Thomistic doctrine. Natural law reasoning is scathingly critiqued by those who allege its intractability and absolutist tendencies,[77] a situation arising from language like this:

> It is therefore evident that, as regards the common principles whether of speculative or of practical reason, truth or rectitude is the same for all, and is equally known by all. But as to the proper conclusions of the speculative reason, the truth is the same for all, but it is not equally known to all. Thus, it is true for all that the three angles of a triangle are together equal to two right angles, although it is not known to all. But as to the proper conclusions of the practical reason, neither is the truth or rectitude the same for all, nor where it is the same, is it equally known by all.[78]

Critics, however, cannot fathom that natural law reasoning only insists that a man act in conformity with what reason instructs. That there is one type of human person—the rational one—is indisputable. Reason commands as natural inclinations enunciate. In this sense, it would be ludicrous to fashion another species of man endowed with another version of reason. Therefore, in human conduct reason rules and commands the other powers, and this universal condition labels permanently the natural law.[79] This unchangeable, immutable reflection of the eternal law, this participation, albeit imperfect, by man in the eternal law, this imprint, messaging inclinations and ends for the human person, is the essence of the natural law.

The Divine Law

Thomas' recognition of the divine exemplar, the divine intellect giving rationality to the universe, and the view that God's very being is the eternal law itself, is often considered the thesis of *divine law*. *Divine law*, while having the qualities of God's rationality and plan, is not the same as the eternal law. *Divine law*, in the most elementary framework, is the Old and New Testaments, which comprise the Bible. It is easy to interchangeably term the *eternal* law the *divine*, and the *divine* the *eternal*, for common parlance often does so. Instead, one finds St. Thomas fully cognizant of the role and purpose of Scripture in the life of the Christian, and that this same Scripture has revelatory qualities. Scripture explains the mind and particular commands of a transcendent, perfect God. Additionally, the eternal, natural and human laws, while interdependent and unified in a teleological sense, do not, according to St. Thomas, directly address the law of salvation. Thomas suggests divine law serves this end:

> [T]he end of the divine law is to bring man to that end which is everlasting happiness; and this end is hindered by any sin, not only of external action, but also of internal action. Consequently, that which suffices for the perfection of human law, viz., the prohibition and punishment of sin, does not suffice for the perfection of the divine law; but it is requisite that it should make man altogether fit to partake of everlasting happiness.[80]

It is obvious that St. Thomas is not just paying lip service as to the divine law's value in his jurisprudence. Heavily and regularly seen throughout his works is a litany of citations to Scripture passages. Jean Tonneau's essential study, *Teaching of the Thomistic Tract on Law*, mathematically computes the number of times St. Thomas utilizes scriptural references in the *Treatise on Law* at *Questions 90* through *108*.[81]

On the other hand, it's quite apparent that St. Thomas' hierarchical coverage of law, the *eternal* to *human* legal continuum, spends less time on the divine law that its temporal counterpart, *human* law. Henle describes this portion of the *Treatise on Law* as "strictly a religious or theological one"[82] and this emphasis is not as frequently confronted in St. Thomas's jurisprudence. In fact, earlier works, like the *Summa Contra Gentiles*, appear to inaccurately distinguish between the categories of *Divine* and *Eternal*. At *Book III* on *Providence*, St. Thomas elevates the *divine* law more than usual, for its word is God's and its source the highest and most perfect good. The end of every law, Thomas declares, including the divine law, is to "make men good."[83] At this stage of his legal analysis, he appears to liberally interchange "eternal" and "divine" law terms. Missing within the *Summa Contra Gentiles* is the natural law's participatory role in God's eternal law, and the distinction between the revelation of God's Testaments and the law of God, the *lex aeterna*. As Thomas' thought matures, the distinction between eternal and divine will be clarified. In the *Treatise on Law*, St. Thomas unassailably depends on God's word, and its integral, central role in the life of the Christian player. It is just this quality of "directing human conduct"[84] that makes divine law central to St. Thomas. Accepting the condition of human frailty and imperfection, realizing the historical evidence for both success and failure on the part of God's people, St. Thomas looks to scriptural instruction as a guide in a world of competing moral claims. When in doubt, God's word can and does resolve dilemmas, legal or otherwise. To assure salvation, God's divine instruction helps man "know without any doubt what he ought to do and what he ought to avoid."[85]

The Human Law

Those less learned about Aquinas often assume that human law is either incidental or deficient when compared to the *eternal*, *natural* and *divine* law. The things of the earth are by no means as lofty or principled as the perfections of God. Nor are the legal musings of man as legislator, lawyer and judge possibly on par with the divine or eternal promulgations. Despite the imperfection, human laws are essential to Thomas' theory of law since their content aims "at the ordering of human life ... under the precepts of a life we have to lead."[86] Moreover, human law maintains its integrative place in Thomistic jurisprudence because of its relation to reality, to social and political living and governance and to the advancement of temporal happiness. Undeniably, human or positive law can never be as comprehensive or as perfect as its relational superiors—the *eternal, natural* and *divine* laws—and if its terminus and enforceability depend solely on its human, secular object, then such a law, if not today, will tomorrow exact an injustice. This inevitable tragedy that results when human law is the centerpiece of a legal system is easy enough to predict. Since *human* law is promulgated by human beings, it will always be subject to error and mistake. Nevertheless, *human* law is driving toward and is concerned with the same goods as its highest counterpart. Law, as previously defined, is an exercise of reason, a *rule and measure* of it. Human laws directly reflect the exercise of practical reason—assessing individual facts and circumstances and then deliberating, enacting, and infusing authority by actual laws. Human laws are not, according to Thomas, the exclusive province of the positivist. Not because man is the author of the human law, but more persuasively because man, in exercising practical reason, entwines himself with the God who fashioned him.[87] It would be grotesquely inaccurate to type Thomas' human law as isolated or independent of its legal counterparts. St. Thomas, in response to whether there is such a thing as the human law, insists on its utility and its unbridled necessity.[88] Human law, is not only language, but the power to habituate, the strength to reign in the unreasonable and the untrue, a prescription for the virtues. Indeed for Thomas, "it is difficult to see how man could suffice"[89] without it.

The Necessity of Human Law

One of the most striking features of Thomas' discussion of human law is its *necessity*—a belief that human existence would fail without legal promulgations. Human beings need commands, proscriptions, and prohibitions to carry out their individual and collective enterprise. Laws serve as a series of parameters and controls for human conduct. Although human beings are fundamentally geared to the good, and by their rational nature can identify proper ends, experience delineates the value of control. Wills, passions and appetites tug and, at times, overwhelm the rational creature that chooses conduct contrary to their nature. Indeed, St. Thomas is bold enough to assert that a morally inclined individual has little need of human law because that person already adheres to the dictates of practical reason, the mandates of the natural law, the divine law precepts and the blueprint of the eternal law. This type of character is rare for the theory of necessity relates to the bulk of humanity.[90] Those already disposed to virtue have less need for legal regulation while those whose "disposition is evil are not led to virtue unless they are compelled."[91]

The *necessity* of human law, as St. Thomas poses, "refers to the removal of evils"[92] from the world we inhabit. Law, in the human sense, is the purifier, the fortress against the onslaught of moral barbarism. From another perspective, the necessity of human law is manifest in human activity of every sort, especially in the communal setting. Positive law involves both the "*law of nations* and *civil law.*"[93]

Neither in anarchy nor in isolation the human person carries out a social and political existence reliant upon law. Henle argues that human law is necessary not because of its own necessity, but because of the "state of fallen man."[94] The law is not inherently coercive, but it's consistent with all its other purposes, "directive" of what ought to be done. To be sure, law has the power to coerce and mold, but since law is a pure exercise of reason, the human actor should be comfortable with its content. Those exercising behavior in accordance with reason are willing properly and thus not in need of coercive power of the law. In this sense "the good are not subject to law, but only the wicked."[95] Hence, human law is necessitous for both reasons of utility and man's current lack of perfection. It is, for lack of better description, a libation that the virtuous can avoid and the wicked must drink.

The Derivative Nature of Human Law

Any legal professional soon discovers that most law has a precedential legacy. Cases of first instance are temporary events, since legal pronouncements eventually attract a following. When enough people praise the decision and enough support is generated amongst the legal community, a legal maxim and principle is borne. To have any credibility, a law withstands the test of time and the clamor of the crowd. Good laws are not drafted in isolation, but rooted in tradition. Human law is derived from other sources including the theological and philosophical underpinnings espoused by St. Thomas. Even speeding, jaywalking, taxes, etc., have a derivative quality, especially in the justness behind their enactment. Kings, too, derive their authority from a higher power, although history is replete with examples of those who turn the crown into an anointing, who would "usurp that right, by framing unjust laws, and by degenerating into tyrants who preyed on their subjects."[96] Human law depends upon and looks to the *eternal, natural* and *divine* laws. Using his integrative method, Thomas finds it impossible to separate human law from the natural law order so evident in rational creatures. At most, Aquinas places human law lower in his legal hierarchy because its enforceability depends upon human beings, while divine law "persuades men by means of rewards or punishments to be received from God. In this respect it employs higher means."[97] Since law is an exercise of human reason, and reason is the *rule and measure* of law, Thomas argues that human law is derived from the natural and eternal law. "Now in all human affairs a thing is said to be just from being right, according to the rule of reason. But the first rule of reason is the law of nature, as is clear from what has been stated above.[98] Consequently, every human law has just so much of the nature of law as it is derived from the law of nature."[99] Since positivism zealously excludes any rootedness beyond its promulgation, it has stripped away, gutted moral inquiry in human law analysis. Rights are based on codifications, the mutterings of "some tiny little minority of an elite,"[100] rather than inherencies or perennial truths.

The derivative relationship between the positive law and "higher" law is not one based on confrontation but one of unity and integration. Human laws that are contrary to the tenets of the natural law, are by implication, an affront to the eternal law, and not really laws in the truest sense. Radically, Thomas holds that *every law* is derived from the eternal law because of reason's role in the deliberation, and a law deviating from reason has not the nature of law in any sense.[101] A human law, inconsistent with the natural, does *violence* to the very notion of what law is and, ergo cannot bind in conscience.[102] Neither, therefore, is it nor can it be law as popularly understood. Human laws inconsistent with the divine law receive no recognition from Thomas since any enactment "contrary to the divine law ... has not the nature of law."[103] Any human promulgation antagonistic to the eternal, divine and natural laws will be an affront to any version of law and equity. To so hold is a radical error in jurisprudence. Thus, Thomas declares "But in so far as it deviates from reason, it is called an unjust law, and has the nature, not of law but of violence."[104]

The *stamp of its ancestry* causes the Thomistic jurist to think teleologically, always searching for the ultimate end of man, that supernatural dimension in the human agent's existence. Though derivative, human law is not a perfect undertaking. Human law, in order to be a sensible human exercise, cannot be expected to eradicate and suppress every act of vice or sin, since men are bound to err. Overzealously enforcing human laws will only produce social resistance and tumult. Thomas is completely opposed to a nation that enslaves its citizens by laws. Too much regulation and control will trigger a revolution of vice and even greater evils will appear. "Therefore it does not lay upon the magnitude of imperfect men the burdens of those who are already virtuous, viz. that they should abstain from all evil. Otherwise these imperfect ones, being unable to bear such precepts, would break out into yet greater evils."[105]

Human law images its author — the human person. Pragmatically, St. Thomas understands the limitations of human promulgations since no human law can plausibly be expected to stamp out human error. It is not only implausible, but presumptive since human law lacks the power to do so. Instead, Thomas suggests recognition of limitations in the use of human law. "Human law likewise does not prohibit everything that is forbidden by the natural law."[106]

On the other hand, the objective of human law is to look to the heavens, and to prod man toward a life of virtue. A Thomist discovers early on that law has a formidable relationship with virtue and that every human law should contribute to the advancement of individual and collective virtue. Law should foster, not inhibit self-perfection.[107]

Human law transforms the citizenry "who live under common legal institutions into perfect citizens."[108] The law, as an instrument of the state, wishes perfection and happiness for its community. The positive or human law cannot possibly extinguish human imperfection in every case, but it can lead men gradually[109] to a life of virtue.

The Nature of Law According to Martin Luther King, Jr.

Any meaningful understanding of King's theory of civil disobedience need initially examine his concept of a law. He had plenty of opportunity to encounter law. When Dr. King sat in jail, the mechanism that delivered him to the jail block was a law of some sort. "Colored" water fountains or counter seats were promulgated by law in many quarters. In a sense, the "law" institutionalized racism at many levels in the American way of life. The very fact that slavery existed at all in a nation grounded in Jeffersonian principles is the ultimate irony. As an illustration, slavery edifies the dilemma—that "law" is either something that humans promulgate or something pertaining to another order. Slavery was possible only because men so legislated. Slavery, at least in a eugenic sense as contrasted with Roman or Greek slavery, is an indefensible proposition. So was the institutionalized and very "legal" extermination of millions of Jews, Slavs, and Gypsies during the horrid Third Reich. In both of these cases, the "law" was very proper and its promulgators endlessly and even slavishly urged the citizen to adhere to its content. The thousands of Catholic priests who challenged the workings of the Hitlerian nightmare, and subsequently perished in the ovens, gas chambers and starvation, fervently understood the inadequacy of this type of law. Herein lays the crux of the matter—to discern what a law really is. Both St. Thomas and Dr. King are left impoverished by the modern penchant for positivism, that view the law is what is says that it is. Dr. King's impassioned plea in *Strength to Love* illustrates this proposition by labeling unjust laws as "unenforceable obligations," that are "beyond the reach of the laws of society."[110] King fully understands the inability of positive law to tackle some of the larger and more meaningful legal and ethical dilemmas. He notes that some obligations concern:

> … Inner attitudes, person-to-person and expressions of compassion which law books cannot regulate and jails cannot rectify. Such obligations are met by one's commitment to an inner law, written in the heart.[111]

King was acutely suspicious of any ideology resting in the exclusivity of man, even arguing that modern "liberalism has presented too shallow a view of man."[112] In positivism, the law has many faces, some good and many ugly. Surely, neither Aquinas nor King would ever claim that human law is not essential to an ordered society. In the Thomistic view, human law plays a central role in the habituation of the citizen. Any short reading of St. Thomas makes plain that law is an essential characteristic of the rational player. Human beings need and must have law since they are rational creatures. Law, for St. Thomas, habituates, teaches and corrals in those who otherwise would run amok without restraint.[113]

But an obsessive and exclusive view of positivism inevitably leads to a corrupt jurisprudence. Positivism is what Dr. King contended with. Human law is what subjected him to a myriad of indignities while simultaneously providing extraordinary possibilities for positive change. Human law provides both remedy and curse in the world of Dr. King. As King dealt with human promulgations that protected a system of inherent inequality, he had to look to a higher form of law in the vein of St. Thomas. It was his anchor in a sea of social turbulence. At its base, King appreciates the inadequacy of human law when dealing with the soul and heart of the human person. No law can force a willing goodness nor change the hard-hearted person into the loving player. Even so, human law has the power to coerce even the unwilling as this power of persuasion can effect change. As King argues:

The law cannot make an employer love an employee but it can prevent him from refusing to hire me because of the color of my skin.[114]

Both King and Aquinas pine for a morality with certitude. In short, some things are right and some things are not. How this certitude impacts law and legislation is something utterly lost on modern legislators and jurists although King never forgets the interplay. King is thoroughly indebted to Aquinas regarding the ethicality of civil disobedience. King realizes that moral relativity is what erected the injustice of racial inequality. In Aquinas, King finds the "Father" of the faith and reason continuum—that recognition that reason per se is inadequate in moral affairs and that faith illumines reason. According to Dr. King, the thought of St. Thomas demonstrates the "harmonious relationship between reason and revelation."[115] In modernism, King sees the tragedy of moral relativism on stage in so many settings. If law purports to be of value, does it not need a moral rationalization or justification? Does the positivist, by promulgation alone, justify? Dr. King would never have been at ease with this scant jurisprudence. Neither would have Aquinas. Law must depend on a fixed series of first principles and propositions. It cannot be right simply because its proponent states that it is or isn't. Law and morality are symbiotically tied together with the caveat that the morality has meaning, not mere terminology. Part of the landscape King contends with arises from a contemporary immorality or amorality that severs laws from these types of perennial questions. Is it right? Is it defensible in a moral sense? What conclusions are self evident and universally applicable? Modern society is awash in decision making devoid of moral reasoning. King applies these concepts in his Sermon, *A Knock at Midnight,*

It is also midnight within the moral order. As midnight colors lose their distinctiveness and become a sullen shade of gray. Moral principles have lost their distinctiveness. For modern man, absolute right and wrong are a matter of what the majority is doing. Right and wrong are relative to likes and dislikes and the customs of a particular community. We have unconsciously applied Einstein's theory of relativity, which properly described the physical universe, to the moral and ethical realm.[116]

In a more particular way, King had to deal with legal issues presently pressing. His decision to deal with injustice provides a laboratory for applied ethics. For example, when King chose to disregard an "injunction" ordering him not to demonstrate publicly[117] regarding segregationist policies, he had to grapple with his historic sense of obligation to the law.[118] King told his followers to adhere to the law as they carried out the cause—and never to engage in conduct that would "criminalize" their enterprise. Early on, Dr. King concluded that his mission must be on the highest possible ground, untouchable as to its ethicality and constructed in the language of love in place of violence and hatred. Referring to his choice of nonviolent resistance as the "proper method"[119] King deduces that "violence is impractical as well as immoral."[120] More specifically, King assessed and analyzed statutory language that is proclaimed "law" but which has another look altogether. In the world of Martin Luther King, law after law reinforcing the segregationist mentality were not only enacted but viewed as obligatory. For King, the blind obedience to law would no longer do. King had to look to a higher plane to justify what he was about to undertake. When describing the philosophy of St. Thomas, King shows his compatibility with an ideology that commences with the temporal and moves "upward from particular things to God."[121] His entire movement had to be rooted in something far more metaphysical. King, as does Aquinas, finds that some laws are just and others are not. In the latter instance, the obligatoriness and binding dissipates. "Fidelity to the law"[122] without consideration for the ethics of the promulgation will not cut it for King. King calls it a sort of "transphysics"[123] which the segregationist and racist perspective simply cannot fathom. When weighing the intentionality of legal and police action during the days of Bull Connor and others, King urges his followers to think in a grander way about these principles. He remarks:

> Bull Connor would next say, "Turn the Fire Hoses on."
> And as I said to you the other night, Bull Connor didn't

know history. He knew a kind of physics that somehow didn't relate to the transphysics we know about. And that fact was there was a certain kind of fire that no water could put out.[124]

There can be no other way for either King or Aquinas since both see that the essential man is composed of more than mere flesh but a "being of spirit"[125] whose presence is "in nature yet above nature...."[126] His metaphysical approach finds full and complete comfort in Christian tradition and Christ himself. King repeatedly and without any equivocation, exhorts his followers to discern the centrality of Christ in all things. Any understanding of law will be meaningless without being viewed in the prism of Christology. History has shown the other reality of brute force, tyranny, military dictatorship and amoral regimes run amuck. King finds no solace in the wasteland of historical experiment but instead discovers eternal comfort in Christ himself. When assessing the sense of Communism, King is caustic about the movement's general emptiness for it forgets what really matters in the human player—a "being of spirit, crowned with glory and honor, endowed with the gift of freedom."[127] At no place will this be truer than his examination and analysis of what law is or should be. As King relates:

> Alexander, Caesar, Charlemagne, have built great empires. But upon what did they depend? They depended upon force. But long ago Jesus started an empire that depended on love, and even to this day millions will die for him.[128]

The fact that slavery and inequality were legally regularized seems astonishing. Yet these systems were along for more than a generational reality. Inequality was legally entrenched in the principles of segregation even though politicians and citizenry in some circles fought its overthrow with extraordinary tenacity. Over time these grave injustices could not brook the truth of things—this notion that a system erected on injustice is bound to fall on its faulty moorings. King holds that an unjust system will suffer the "inevitable decay of any system based on principles that are not in harmony with the moral laws of the universe."[129] Even the American experience manifests a conceptual understanding of these principles but an applied understanding that runs far field. America, deeply indebted to its Judeo-Christian heritage, King argues, is a "marvelous foundation for any home."[130] Take, for example, the 2009 presidential race, where President-Elect Barack Obama is soon to corroborate how truth eventually replaces error. Despite the glorious platitudes that "all men are made in the image of God; every man is an heir to a legacy of dignity and worth; all men are created equal,"[131] America has "strayed away."[132]

Chapter 2

Defining Civil Disobedience

Introduction

The term *civil disobedience* elicits many connotations and definitions. To disobey, in the most general sense, implies some sort of defiance or unlawful activity. To disobey means that the human agent chooses, with both will and intent, to disregard some rule or restriction. Disobedience in any form is generally frowned upon in a civil society, whether it emanates from family or school or community to a nation state. Coupling the word "civil" to disobedience expresses another dimension in this puzzle—since it is here that the citizen, residing and living in the community, chooses to disregard a promulgated law. Thus, the disobedience is carried out by ordinary citizens who object to the legitimacy of a law.

There are various forms of this disobedience—the absolute version—where the moral player rejects not only the legitimacy of the law but also its capacity to be labeled or defined as a law. In this case, the party disobeying refuses recognition of an unjust law. In the other case, the disobeying agent tags a law as unjust although begrudgingly accepts the nature of its promulgation. Here the critic concludes that laws can be either bad or good yet still exist under the rubric called law. The first variety of which we speak constitutes the radical version of civil disobedience and it mirrors, with perfect accuracy, the jurisprudence of St. Thomas Aquinas. His civil disobedience theory will simultaneously hold that a "law lacking moral legitimacy is not legally valid,"[1] and, as moral beings and citizens, we are obliged to disobey it and work for its repeal.[2] St. Thomas' natural law theory will be the barometer of whether any law can pass muster, since the power of the natural law rests in its capacity to "check the legitimacy of human-made laws."³

Seven centuries later, Dr. Martin Luther King, Jr. will weigh the righteousness of an entire movement set on changing segregation. How could he justify a movement that massively disobeyed the established order? How did he define civil disobedience and what criteria justified the many tactics of agitation and interruption in the normal flow of events in the community? For Dr. King, the question of disobedience did not arise from petty events or trivial disagreements but with the broad issues of human rights and equality as these pertain to specific laws and ordinances. To illustrate, whether a person drinks from a particular water fountain, sits in the front or the back of a bus, eats food in seats categorized by race or color, appear at first glance, to be not the stuff of major resistance. Yet these injustices are particular examples of the gross injustice of segregation and the larger issue of equality. In the smaller injustices once discerns the grander, negative impacts of a discriminatory society. It is in this laboratory of specific human events that the legitimacy of civil disobedience gets tested. In this sense, the disobedience takes on a civil quality—in that it deals with some human promulgation, some regulation involving the general citizenry. Hence, civil disobedience resides in two domains—first, the idea that the agent chooses to disobey fully realizing the nature of the disobedience, and second, that the subject matter or basis for the choice of civil disobedience rests in human affairs. Put another way, civil disobedience demands more than just a philosophy or a theoretical juxtaposition on human action, but rather requires a specific activity that represents the basis of the disobedience. One cannot civilly disobey in mind alone. Mind must be coupled with human action—whether the disobedience be in the form of public protest, a refusal to move or in the public square, a rejection of some policy or practice, or a deliberate refusal to cooperate with public authority. The mode of action in civil disobedience cannot be fully catalogued since action will depend on the nature of the injustice or moral objection posed by the party who disobeys. In sum, any meaningful description of civil disobedience will depend on two factors; namely, the subject matter prompting the disobedience

2 · DEFINING CIVIL DISOBEDIENCE

and the action chosen to demonstrate resistance. This is civil disobedience in its most elementary form. However, this assessment is woefully inadequate in the world of both St. Thomas and Dr. King. At the forefront, how does one know that a law is unjust and not worthy of our obedience? What characteristics make for the just law and conversely what traits constitute the unjust law? What standards or criteria do we measure with or apply to existing legal dilemmas? Does civil disobedience depend on some moral order that is objective rather than subjective?

Justice or Injustice in a Law

A proponent of civil disobedience must initially assess the justness or injustice of a particular law. Civil disobedience expressly requires a moral righteousness in human affairs and this finding implies more than just mere opinion. Obviously a just law would not be the proper target for the advocate since just laws are in accord with proper ends.[4] In short, bona fide civil disobedience must initially determine whether a law is just or not. In the first instance, just laws bind, as St. Thomas would say,

> Laws framed by men are either just or unjust. If they be just, they have the power of binding in conscience, from the eternal law from whence they are derived.[5]

The term "bind" can also be described as "oblige." Allegiance and adherence to any law depends upon this initial inquiry for a just law need be followed and in contrast, the "unjust" law need be resisted and even overturned. King fully understands this dynamic when he remarks:

> One has not only a legal a moral responsibility to obey just laws. Conversely, one has a moral responsibility to disobey unjust laws.[6]

It is no secret that Martin Luther King, Jr. heavily relies on the jurisprudence of Aquinas. He clearly holds,

A just law is a manmade code that squares with the moral
law or the law of God. An unjust law is a code that is out
of harmony with the moral law. To put it in the terms of
St. Thomas Aquinas: An unjust law is a human law that
is not rooted in the eternal or natural law.[7]

In his *Letter from the Birmingham Jail*,[8] King authors his most
sophisticated correlation between just and unjust laws. King dis-
sects segregation laws with extraordinary clarity. From one position, he cannot understand how any enactment, which excludes a
group on color or race grounds, can be anything but unjust, for a
just "law is a code that a majority compels a minority to follow and
that it is willing to follow itself."[9] While Dr. King cites the me-
dievalist perspective on the unjust law, he tends to be more contemporary and humanistic in his analysis. On more than one oc-
casion, King labels the unjust law as something "dehumanizing"
and "degrading."[10] Susan Tiefenbrun argues that King's jurisprudence uses "several different metaphoric codes: religious, psychological and legal."[11] In another way, King creatively describes how
laws can appear just, at least textually, yet can be unjust "in its application."[12] He uses the example of a rightful permit requirement
—this being just on its face, yet unjust when arbitrarily or capri-
ciously denied in order to maintain or advance segregation policy.

King, as Aquinas, looks to the law's impact on the human personality, but does he do so in a less theoretical way? Will Aquinas
query whether the law directs the citizen to the good, to virtue, to
proper ends? King will more broadly ask whether the law uplifts
the human condition. King's view of justice tends to incorporate
economic, political and social factors in the mix as if at street level.
Does a person have opportunity, and if not, why? King ties together the material with the metaphysical when describing justice
in *I Have a Dream*.

In a sense we've come to our nation's capital to cash a
check. When the architects of our republic wrote the magnificent words of the Constitution and the Declaration of
Independence, they were signing a promissory note to
which every American was to fall heir. This note was a

promise that all men, yes black men as well as white men, would be guaranteed the 'unalienable Rights to Life, Liberty and the pursuit of Happiness.' It is obvious today that America has defaulted on this promissory note insofar as her citizens of color are concerned. Instead of honoring this sacred obligation, America has given the Negro a bad check, a check which has come back marked 'insufficient funds.'

But we refuse to believe that the bank of justice is bankrupt.[13]

When assessing the justness of segregation laws, King argues from multiple fronts as to why the laws are not worthy of our obedience.

Any law that uplifts the human personality is just. Any law that degrades human personality is unjust. All segregation statutes are unjust because segregation distorts the soul and damages the personality. It gives the segregator a false sense of superiority and the segregated a false sense of inferiority.[14]

For St. Thomas only a just law is worthy of our obedience. If not, it need not be followed and in a sense the Christian has an affirmative duty to rid the common good of this type of promulgation. St. Thomas lays out a very elaborate theory of justice in relation to law—a jurisprudence of the "right." Commencing with the perfect justice, God the Creator, St. Thomas lays out a definitional and essential blueprint for the notion of justice. These conceptual principles will influence Dr. King in multiple ways as his movement unfolds.

As in all other aspects of Thomas' work, *justice* is an eclectic concept, inexorably finding its meaning in teleology from God to man, from perfection to imperfection, from the ultimate, purest goods to temporal ones.[15] God, the eternal lawmaker, consists of pure and perfect justice. Just laws are consistent with the divine exemplar and unjust laws are an affront to this perfection. Hence, the justice of any law is derived from its relationship to its end, the common good, the legitimacy of the lawmaker, from its form and sensibility, its proportionality and equity.[16] Derivatively, the lawfulness and justness of human activity descend from God's justice. Thomas proclaims that the "order of justice arises by relation to the first cause, who is the ruler of all justice."[17] In a more concrete sense, justice provides a measure for legislation and is characterized in four fundamental ways. First, justice is a rational exercise while its counterpart, injustice, is contrary to reason. Second, justice is a virtuous disposition, an habituation, in which the human actor gives both citizen and community what is *due*. Third, justice is generally a measure of the mean in human conduct—that balance of behavior and result that keeps interrelationships and political and communal entities in balance. Finally, St. Thomas categorizes justice by its forms: *distributive* and *commutative*.

Indeed, any Thomistic insight on justice immediately appreciates the interrelationship between a state and an individual that is just or unjust. Thomas firmly believes that the lifeblood of person and people depend on justice for "it is of the essence of a nation that the mutual relations of the citizens be ordered by just laws."[18] No place is this position more apparent than in Thomas' suggestion that unjust laws, the promulgations crafted contrary to reason, the natural law, and the divine and eternal laws, are really illusory enactments.[19] Unjust laws lack an obligatory force and should be disregarded, attacked as injurious to the common and individual good, and in a way, disobeyed. Legitimacy, enforceability and obligatoriness do not arise because a *law* is a *law*.

What is so consistently evident in Thomas' treatment of justice is its relational quality. Justice cannot exist, in the human sphere, without others, and is about "external actions and things,"[20] about operations not passions,[21] and unlike charity, which supremely envelops all the virtues, it is especially concerned with relational interaction. Justice is about external operations and activities, whether person or governmental entity. Giving each his or her due "according to equality of proportion"[22] is the proper act of justice. Justice is, as Macintyre interprets Thomas, relational and communal, "To every human being every other human being thus owes, and of all the virtues *iustitia* is the one peculiarly concerned with relations to others."[23] And this rough conclusion applies to the ruling hierarchy as well for in the mind of Thomas rulers should rule with not only justice in mind, but all the virtues and just as critically peace and happiness in the collective. Jaime Velez-Saenz sums up this proposition with keen insight,

> St. Thomas insists repeatedly that the ruler should strive to promote peace, and even states that this should be his main purpose. And this assertion is in agreement with the preeminent function he assigns in the social life to the unity of all his parts in order to act, so it is only when united by the link of peace that the multitude can be conducted to the virtuous operation which is happiness.[24]

Justice as the Mean

Continuing the Aristotelian conception of virtue,[25] Thomas sees justice, as well as other virtues, in measurable terms, particularly the *mean*—that balance of intellect, appetites and passions, reason and will, that behavioral modicum representing the human agent doing what is in accord with nature and reason. The mean, in most cases, is neither mathematical nor political. Justice "is a mean between having too much and too little."[26] Compromise is not the mean as if the moral agent could choose conduct if only in reasonable amounts. Nor is the mean an avoidance of extremes, e.g., the drunkard versus the prohibitionist, the chaste versus the promiscuous. Thomistic psychology is more multidimensional. The *mean* is only discoverable when evaluated in light of human reason and rationality. Thomas states:

> Moral virtue derives its goodness from the rule of reason, while its matter consists in passions or operations. If therefore, we compare moral virtue to reason, and then if we look at that which it has of reason, it holds the position of one extreme, viz., conformity; while excess and defect take the position of the other extreme, viz., deformity. But if we consider moral virtue in respect of its matter, then it has the nature of a mean, in so far as it makes the passion conform to the rule of reason.[27]

Both excess and defect of reason disregard the mean. Every virtue, whether temperance, prudence, fortitude, etc., directs itself towards a specific object, and to be properly called a virtue, the measure of its quality as virtue is its "conformity to reason."[28] Gilson illustrates the mean of any intellectual virtue as truth since it "is the just mean, determined by the thing itself. And it is this very truth which confers moral excellence upon a virtue."[29] The mean consists not of political accommodation but a balance, an accord with natural traits, attributes and dispositions. On the other hand, justice's mean is calculated using the external dynamic, consisting "in a certain proportion of equality between the external thing and the external person."[30]

Justice's elemental concern with equality, proportionality and equity leads Thomas to conclude that justice's mean is more or less "arithmetical"[31] when compared to the means of other virtues. Justice is about commerce, crime and punishment, political authority and citizenry, property and ownership, distribution of money and usury. "Justice, then, is a virtue whereby men fulfill their judicial obligations."[32] Its operative quality imputes a relational, interpersonal rationality, Thomas claims. "The reason for this is that justice is about operations, which deal with external things, wherein the right has to be established absolutely and in itself,…. Hence the mean of reason in justice is the same as the real mean, in so far, namely, as justice gives to each one his due, neither more nor less."[33] For example, to sustain and preserve a friendship, that emotional bond between persons requires a "proportionate return"[34] of thoughts, emotions and interpersonal acts. In other words, the mean of justice cannot be determined without reference to others.

Justice is also conformity, balance and equilibrium, in stark contrast to "injustice, deformity, discordance and inequality."[35] Thomas' articulation of what constitutes justice's mean, is foundationally tied to reason itself. "Law is reason ordaining what must be done to bring about justice, i.e., the just, or, the right. It tells us how equality, that is to say, a proper commensuration, ought to be achieved, what the *debitum* is, and how it should be rendered. Our enduring desire to render what is due another is the virtue of justice; the enactment of rules whereby the *debitum* will be recognized and rendered is part of the virtue of prudence—its legislative aspect."[36] Within every aspect of virtue analysis, Thomas enumerates reason as the *rule and measure* of existence. So the mean of justice is "also the rational mean."[37] Wanting too much, craving, envying, avariciously desiring what others have is antagonistic to justice, as is hatred toward the races, prejudice and stereotyping as well as the craven inequality touted as lawful in the world of civil rights.

The Nature of Injustice

To further explain justice, Thomas expends energy cataloguing the nature of *injustice*. *Injustice* is contrary and confrontational to the rational mean; it is disproportionate and defamatory, zealously desiring or inordinately possessing. Thomas calls injustice a "special"[38] form of vice because it negatively influences both the individual actor and society. Individual acts of injustice that taint the sanctity of the multitude are repugnant to the common good, and such "contempt of the common good may lead to all kinds of sins."[39] Wisely, Thomas suggests that individual injustices negatively affect an entire community. So convinced of injustice's severity and its opposition to Thomas' rational mean, he terms any act of injustice a *mortal* sin.[40] Injustice is classified as not only an irrational act, but one that can only be involuntarily accepted since the human agent never yearns for injustice, and "no man suffers an injustice except against his will."[41] It is therefore inconsistent with our nature to desire injustice, nor to willingly heap it upon our being. For St. Thomas, even choosing to do an unjust thing is more difficult than doing justice. "It is not easy for any man to do an unjust thing from choice, as though it were pleasing for its own sake and not for the sake of something else."[42]

The Forms of Justice

While justice is to give each man his due, justice is "suitably assigned"[43] depending upon circumstances. Thomas, as Aristotle, divides justice into two basic species: 1) *commutative* and 2) *dis-*

tributive, and when either of these is applied to a communal setting, he further differentiates into *legal justice*. Thomas defines commutative justice in a relational sense, between two individuals or between individuals and particular groups. *Commutative* justice's chief concern is the reciprocity, the equality between people and circumstance. Concerned more with strict equality than its distributive counterpart this form of justice "governs man's civil intercourse and thus by far the greater part of his social life."[44] *Commutative* justice, with its emphasis on equality, encompasses the equilibrium, the reaction to action, the price for the product. *Commutative* justice fosters individual tranquility and peace and is an indispensable condition of social existence.

In his *Commentary on Aristotle's Ethics*, Thomas relates how parties are voluntarily involved " ... *in selling and buying*, in *barter*, in *bail*, in *a loan, in a deposit*, in *rent*."[45] Voluntary transactions are just, while involuntary ones "like theft, by which one takes a thing belonging to another who is unwilling; adultery, by which a man secretly approaches the wife of another for sexual intercourse; poisoning, by which a person poisons another with intent either to kill or injure in some way"[46] are unjust. Segregation laws are inherently unjust due to their involuntary nature. No person wishes or desires unequal status nor would any citizen crave for secondary status or a diminution of rights when compared to others based on artificial criteria. Commutative justice gives each what he or she is due. Thomas terms this type of justice as *equalizing*. "Hence it is necessary to equalize thing with thing, so that the one person should pay back to the other just so much as he has become richer out of that which belonged to the other. The result of this will be equality according to the *arithmetical mean* which is gauged according to equal excess in quantity."[47]

Commutative justice is therefore about "mutual dealings." Segregation and racial inequality cannot achieve the fundamental goal of Thomistic justice.

In the second designation, *distributive*, Thomas reviews the relation between individual action and that of the state, the community, and the societal whole. *Distributive* justice perceives individual identities not in a contractual, egalitarian sense, but more as a citizen in the collective, who may or may not have more or less than others, whose status may be higher or lower, whose power, governance, or legal authority may differ. Instead of an arithmetical mean, Thomas says that this type of justice is "geometrical."[48] "Hence in distributive justice the mean is observed, not according to equality between thing and thing, but according to proportion between things and persons: in such a way that even as one person surpasses another, so that which is given to one person surpasses that which is allotted to another."[49] In this sense, racial inequality would only be relevant as to unjust distribution — that is when goods, services, honors, powers and privileges are assigned on arbitrary and capricious grounds. To illustrate, political positions that exclude a racial category or group by creed would directly counter the distributive mentality. So much of the Civil Rights Movement was rooted in this form of injustice since exclusion and class differentiation was the prime motivation in the laws that targeted select groups. For Aquinas and King, such laws smack the sensibility of distribution.

Distribution of goods, services, material possessions, political positions, will be neither uniform nor identical, but proportionate to what each is due. *Distributive* justice resists any redistribution of goods, services and authority, but is at ease with a diversity of stations in life. There is nothing unjust about differences, Thomas says, because "in distributive justice a person receives all the more of the common goods, according as he holds a more prominent position in the community."[50] Differences do not imply a disproportionate sharing of resources. In fact, Thomas insists on basic distributions for each citizen.[51] Unreasonable and disproportionate "burdens in taxation or military, partiality and favoritism in public appointments, in the award of honors or of grants of public funds, are incompatible with distributive justice."[52] For example, "payment for laborious work"[53] is expected, while the involuntary forfeiture or taking of property[54] is condemned. *Distributive* justice obliges the state to socially contract with its citizenry. If this is not done, and the individual citizen is left in a state of material and personal neglect, theft is excused. Thomas views human necessaries as subject to communal ownership. If the need is urgent enough, criminal culpability is not present. It is even "lawful" to take either "openly or secretly"[55] to satisfy these fundamental human needs.[56] "Distributive Justice orders the relationship between individuals or groups of individuals and the whole community or the state. It has to do with the distribution of goods, benefits, burdens, etc. to the citizens of the state. This type of Justice regulates the sharing in the Common Good."[57] Doubtless, Thomas presumes fundamental governmental protections for its citizenry, some coherent and equitable distribution of what is materially available to the individual rank and file. A state that neglects its individual citizens primordial needs, is not a just state. Jean Porter intelligently summarizes Thomas' account of distributive justice. "Distributive justice, on the other hand, preserves the proper proportion between what an individual deserves from the community, and what he receives from it."[58]

In either category of justice, the harm inflicted by the scourge of discrimination and race hatred, the human affronts that run side by side with prejudice and racial inequality, and the systematic, institutionalized practices inherent in so many quarters of a slave and quasi slave culture, the standards relative to justice fail. In commutation, the goal rests in essential equality—that man is man despite artificial differences regarding race, creed or color. There can be no justice in any law that promotes inequality in things and essences that equal by nature. Commutative justice demands an equality of sameness though not necessarily identical results. In Thomas' theory of commutative justice, the injustice of race inequality could not be clearer. The right to be free from intrusive injustice does not come about because some legislator thinks up the right so to speak or because some lawyer advocates successfully or a judge rules correctly. Questions of justice and injustice, especially as regards the hideous institution of slavery and historical discrimination, cannot be assessed in light of human argument alone. The very existence of slavery, considering its lifespan and irrational defense, attests to the loss of just reasoning in the affairs of men. For more than a century the American landscape contortedly justified and rationalized crystalline error. For more than a century, legislators and lawmakers, judges and jurists bent common sense, common wisdom and self-evident propositions in distorted positions unrecognizable to the thinking creature. For more than a century, a nation founded on high sounding principles of equality, neglected "a higher authority that embodies both morality and rationality."[59] Raymond Dennehy understands this modern fallacy—that justice depends on the codification or promulgation alone, that a law is law because of its mechanical enactment,

> The Nuremberg Trials and the United Nations condemnation of genocide testify to the reality of that moral revulsion. To commit murder, to interfere with a man's freedom of conscience, to obstruct his freedom to seek the truth, etc., all this is to violate the natural order, and, consequently, to outrage reason. For such actions use a being who is an end in himself as a mere means to an end, as a mere object of scientific or social purpose. In other works, the claim that certain rights, such as the right to life, are natural follows from the conclusion that they are due to a human being because of what he is naturally, i.e., by essence, and not because of what society chooses to allow him.[60]

As for the distributive form of justice, institutionalized racism goes hand and hand with injustice. In racism, there can be no equality of opportunity, no chance for progress on a level playing field, and no recognition of fundamental equality in the human being. Segregation laws fail to "promote human needs and foster a general state of well being."[61] By blocking access and erecting artificial barriers based on race and color, the law seeking this end, can only be typed unjust. If the purpose of law is to assure liberty, any action that undermines this pursuit runs contrary to the idea of law. Law needs to lead men and women to their proper end, to "attain the end for which he was created, of guiding him that he might not select means which would rather divert him from this end."[62]

Finally, it is readily apparent that justice depends on more than mere intentions but an evaluation, consideration and choice of human action relative to some object or good. Only human agents are capable of justice or injustice because only man as a "person has the requisite faculty of rational will."[63] "Justice alone, of all the virtues, implies the notion of duty."[64] When the actor is habituated to the proper object or end of justice—the good, the just, the true and the right live deeply in the conscience of men.

The Method of Civil Disobedience: Non-Violence

Once the determination concerning the injustice of a law has been made, one need consider the steps to challenge and assure the law's demise. Those engaging in civil disobedience consciously weigh a series of actions—though whatever the course of conduct chosen, it tends to the non-violent. Non-violence constitutes the moral center of the civil disobedience even though other avenues of behavior are available. Certainly, violence is a frequently chosen remedy in the war on injustice although there is "less moral authority to support violence rather than subversion...."[65] The American Civil War unfortunately descended into the tragedy of violence since its proponents felt that no other options were realistic. "Belief in the moral righteousness of violence as a means of protesting and changing unjust laws is at least as old as the United States of America."[66] King understood the connection between protest, both the violent and nonviolent variety, and the development of the American psyche.

> We feel that there are moral laws in the universe, just as valid and basic as man-made laws, and whenever a man-made law is in conflict with what we consider the law of God, or the moral law of the universe, then we feel we have a moral obligation to protest. And this is an American tradition all the way from the Boston Tea Party, on down. We have praised individuals in America who stood up with creative initiative to revolt against unjust systems. So that is what we are doing.[67]

During King's time, violent change was advocated in the radical arm of the Civil Rights movement. After years of inequality, after efforts to mainstream, some sectors in the black community saw no other way to achieve equality.[68] Yet, despite this option, and despite its efficacy in select circumstances, traditional schools of civil disobedience do not adhere to violence. King "insisted non-violence is good, and violence is evil, pure and simple."[69] For the advocate of civil disobedience seeks change without injury or harm, desires not a full scale revolution by any means but a reformation of hearts and minds. King desires a society rooted in love and charity, a "beloved community"[70] rather than a culture built on violence and hatred.

St. Thomas, when dwelling on what to do with the tyrant, in the most extreme cases, seems sympathetic, though troubled by the destruction of the tyrant. His language in *On Kingship* displays ambivalence.

> If the excess of tyranny is unbearable, some have been of the opinion that it would be an act of virtue for strong men to slay the tyrant and espouse themselves to the danger of death in order to set the multitude free.[71]

While at first glance, St. Thomas sounds a little comfortable with violent overthrow; his later language suggests attentiveness to the Christian obligation.

> But this opinion is not in accord with apostolic teaching. For Peter admonishes us to be reverently subject to our masters, not only the good and gentle but also the forward. 'For if one who suffers unjustly bears his trouble for conscience sake, this is grace.'[72]

Hence the method of civil disobedience is preemptively non-violent according to Aquinas. St. Thomas displays a realistic streak when he insists that the citizen, even one who lives in an unjust society, must grin and bear it. He calls this type of rule a "mild tyranny,"[73] in which the resistance is not worth the effort or the collateral effects of exerting it. By collateral, we mean the damage to the collective, the tranquility of the community. In other words, the upheaval resulting from the disobedience is simply not worth the price of the disobedience since it causes "perils more grievous."[74] From another angle, St. Thomas warns us that the grass is not always greener in matters of civil disobedience. Be careful what you wish for since the reform may be worse than the status quo—one tyrant for another so to speak with the second version oppressing "his subjects with an even more grievous slavery."[75] In many respects, Aquinas urges the citizen to understand that civil disobedience has a price—sometimes worth the sacrifice; other times not. The cause must be more than inconvenience or disagreement. The cause must, of course, be one rooted in justice. Does, Dr. King queries, the civil disobedience have "the ability to achieve purpose."[76] Violence may add insult to injury and mimic the injustice the advocate seeks to eliminate. Mark DeForrest poetically describes the intentionality,

> Civil disobedience has as its goal, not the destruction of the social order, but its reform or, to use utopianistic language, purification. Civil disobedience attempts to awaken the government, and the majority of society, to a right understanding of justice and the common good.[77]

Critics of civil disobedience often label the practice as lawlessness which could lead society into chaos.[78] The argument usually goes as follows: if Citizen A chooses to disregard Law B what constraint might there be for Citizen B as to Law C? The civil disobedience solely rests on individual leanings and tends to anarchy, it is claimed. Critics generally forget that the jurisprudence of both King and Aquinas rests on divine moorings. Instead of the rabble out of control, picking and choosing which law to abide by and which to disregard, both posit a civil disobedience of human dignity and of first principles. In *Letter from the Birmingham Jail*, King outlines the dilemma:

> In no sense do I advocate evading or avoiding the law, as would the rabid segregationist. That would lead to anarchy. One who breaks an unjust law must do so openly, lovingly, and with a willingness to accept the penalty. I submit that an individual who breaks a law that conscience tells him is unjust, and who willingly accepts the

penalty of imprisonment in order to arouse the conscience of the community over its injustice, is in reality
expressing the highest respect for the law.[79]

In this way, King is very much like Aquinas who incessantly argued that a law is only a law if it is just. Unjust laws fail to oblige,
are incapable of forcing internal adherence and are not worthy of
the designation "law" and because of this conclusion, civil disobedience cannot run amok. Within the jurisprudence of St. Thomas
one must set specific parameters to determine whether a law is a law
at all. St. Thomas holds that the "force of any law depends on the
extent of its justice."[80] And this deduction is driven by the enactment's compatibility with the eternal and natural law. For King, the
law must elevate the human person; recognize the dignity of the
human agent and square with the moral and divine law. As a result,
the advocate picks civil disobedience when all the stars are aligned
so to speak. James P. Hanigan types King's jurisprudence as one
which differentiates the "enforceable" from the "unenforceable."[81]
The legitimacy of civil disobedience arises from a higher order, "the
moral law of the universe, or from love, all of which stand at the
beginning of action not the end."[82] As a result, principles of civil
disobedience only apply in enforceable situations such as equality,
human dignity and preservation of life. It is the nonviolence that
provides the mettle to withstand challenge. It is nonviolence that
provides "discipline"[83] to the movement. In addition, King is never
apologetic concerning his rejection of violence and chides those who
believe that being nonviolent is any easier. King refers to his method
as "spiritually aggressive" rather than "physically aggressive."[84]

In this way, civil disobedience does not wish revolution but
change. Hanigan describes King's approach as a "type of reform
activity rather than the revolutionary overthrow of a system."[85] Violence is usually associated with revolutions and neither Dr. King
nor Aquinas desire any part of that legacy. In the world of St.
Thomas, the resistance to violence was all the more remarkable.
The Middle Ages were not known for pacifist tendencies—the
penchant for war and battle was quite obvious. St. Thomas exerted
extraordinary effort in enveloping his legal theory, his jurispru-

dence in the Christian concept of love. Nothing he argues will be severed from the Gospel, from the eternal God, "since all power is from the Lord God."[86]

Intention in Civil Disobedience

Another measure regarding the legitimacy of civil disobedience is the intentionality of the advocate. Both King and Aquinas impute and insist upon an intent that is correctly motivated and driven by a "higher law" mentality. Civil disobedience does not adequately rest in mere choice or individual preference. In order that it might be defensible, the actor must not only be justified but also keenly aware of the goodness of the cause. Hence the actor is more than the member of a mob demonstrating about this or that, or a protester using civil disobedience as a means to some other end beyond the scope of the protest action. Instead the party engaged in civil disobedience needs to operate from proper motives and a clean heart, and mostly out of love. James Hanigan relays the primacy of love in King's argument for civil disobedience.

> The place that love occupies indicates how deeply and fundamentally religious King's conception of nonviolence was, and clearly marks it off from a purely pragmatic nonviolence that can only seek justification from the results it achieves.[87]

Love signifies a motivation grounded in the good, not strict self interest or advancement. For the actor who loves his neighbor, who witnesses injustice and moves to eradicate it, operates with the type of intentionality necessary for legitimate civil disobedience. Love says so much about the actor especially when compared to the motivation of hate and anger. King's speech, *The Power of Non-Violence*, eloquently describes the motive of a person acting in pure love and charity.

> But when we speak of loving those who oppose us we're not talking about *eros*. The Greek language talks about *philia* and this is a sort of reciprocal love between personal

friends. This is a vital, valuable love. But when we talk of loving those who oppose you and those who seek to defeat you we are not talking about *eros* or *philia*. The Greek language comes out with another word and it is *agape*. *Agape* is understanding, creative, redemptive good will for all men. Biblical theologians would say it is the love of God working in the minds of men. It is an overflowing love which seeks nothing in return.[88]

In love comes salvation of the mind, body and soul. In love there is a recognition that each person has worth and beauty. In love the advocate sits firmly in higher law intentionality rather than the misery of revenge and retribution. King weighed and evaluated this option and chose wisely,

> I have also decided to stick to love … I'm talking about a strong demanding love … And I say to myself that hate is too great a burden to bear. I have decided to love.[89]

His theory of love and correlation to civil disobedience is not "narcissism at large, but an embrace of God's embodied image reflected in the mirror."[90]

The designation, "charity" is often used interchangeably. Charity is the greatest of all virtues according to St. Thomas because it can increase exponentially, cannot be contained and the most apt descriptor—that God is love. Thomas relays:

> Charity consists of in an extreme with regard to its object, in so far as its object is the Supreme Good, and from this it follows that Charity is the most excellent of the virtues.[91]

Thomas recognizes that love and charity provide the moral rationale for any jurisprudence and the particular acts peculiar to it. Love, he states, is capable of continuous addition and improvement; it is infinite, perfect, orderly,[92] and tends "to God as to the principle of happiness…."[93]

Adopting love as the mantra in any movement is no easy task for it requires the human agent to love even those who stand in opposition. When one "loves thy enemy" it is a fair implication that a great deal of thought has taken place. To love those out to hurt and hate insists that the actor choose a course of conduct that is the hardest to pick. Most people either avoid or confront those who are designated enemies. Aquinas delivers a sophisticated way in which we must love our enemies in all cases, though not in all circumstances. As to our natures, that man is man, that type of love must be unconditional. As to what man does or deliberates about, is something altogether different. Here St. Thomas prophetically sees the dilemma of loving the sinner but hating the sin.

> … love of one's enemies may mean that we love them as to their nature, but in general, and in this sense charity requires that we should love our neighbors, namely that in loving God and our neighbor, we should not exclude our enemies from the love given to our neighbor in general.[94]

Another way of looking at intent and motivation relates to the "higher" versus "lower" values continuum. For those legitimately engaging in civil disobedience, the arguments tend to the metaphysical rather than the temporal—even though the problems are here and now. Put another way, the justification usually relies more upon spiritual grounds than earthly ones. This is clearly evident in King's entire mission for his mind, his intent always and without exception, gazes towards the divine horizon. Early in his public career he will remark:

> We cannot be truly Christian people so long as we flaunt the central teachings of Jesus: brotherly love and the Golden Rule.[95]

His mission never depends on what he or anyone else thinks but what a higher order demands. This reliance on the supernatural is surely not a given for other approaches from strict self-interest and power promotion, radical revolutionary tactics to economic demands are commonly adopted. Throughout his entire movement, King exhorts, enlists, solicits and entreats God and in a wide variety of contexts, his son, Jesus Christ. "This conception of God as both good and power for King the substance of what Jesus of

Nazareth has revealed to humankind and it is through his life that we know this about God most definitively. The place and the meaning of Jesus of Nazareth in King's view of human life, is therefore, quite important."[96] King concludes that Jesus Christ is "both a model for life and an inspiration for life."[97] The centrality of Christ says much about the mind of King as it does in Aquinas. In Jesus, Aquinas holds, man may mediate with God for the Christ Jesus alone,

> ... is the perfect Mediator of God and men, inasmuch as, by His Death, he reconciled the human race to God. Hence the Apostle, Mediator of God and man, the man Christ Jesus, added: Who gave Himself for the redemption of all.[98]

Thus both King and Aquinas are joined to God by the Savior and with the salvific act of the Passion, Christ opens the divine domain to the entire world.

Open, Visible and Willing to Suffer

Civil disobedience demands much from its advocates. Civil disobedience is a visible, public and open activity rather than clandestine or secret in design. The party choosing to disobey is fully aware that the disobedience is carried out to raise awareness in a collective sense. Civil disobedience seeks to educate the public about injustice and "awaken the conscience of society by showing society that a law is unjust."[99] In the most extreme sense, the actor must be willing to not only act, but also suffer the consequences of the action. For a person engaged in civil disobedience recognizes the higher legitimacy of their action while simultaneously realizing that their conduct may result in arrest, fine or imprisonment. Put another way, the actor knows the legitimacy of their resistance and is readily willing to accept the consequence. As a result the actor acts with a confidence natural to moral certainty. The actor carries out the disobedience in an open, public and highly visible manner. The civil disobedience, whether it be sit ins, blockage of access or exit, a refusal to comply with a dispersal order, or a neglect of some official requirement, all manifest the public and open nature of civil disobedience. Each of these examples edifies how public action comports with a private conscience that understands justice or injustice in any law. Aquinas is utterly emphatic on our affirmative obligation to deny the legitimacy of any law inconsistent with the eternal and natural law, and logically, one concludes that action, of the public variety, is mandatory. An example from the *Summa Theologica* lays out this duty,

> This argument is true of laws that are contrary to the commandments of God, which is beyond the scope of human power. Wherefore to such matters human law should not be obeyed.[100]

Here, the language posed by St. Thomas firmly prioritizes the higher law of God and then mandates that any human invention contrary to it cannot bind nor does it need our recognition as law. The implications of this non-recognition permit a rejection of state authority. Consider the governmental demand that abortion be provided despite the inconsistency with his higher law philosophy. Aquinas instructs the citizen to disregard the command or promulgation. Aquinas radically recommends rejection and disobedience. None of these suggestions can be done in private. None of these urgings can avoid public scrutiny and in fact pierce the public veil. One cannot resist without taking a stand so to speak or drawing a line somewhere. Others have to know your position and others will be made aware of the purpose behind the disobedience.

On a second front, St. Thomas wants the world to know of his objection to unjust laws and that the Christian citizen must work against these unjust promulgations.

> On the other hand laws may be unjust in two ways: first, by being contrary to human good ... either in respect to the end, as when an authority imposes on his subjects burdensome laws, conducive, not to the common good, but rather for his own cupidity or vainglory;—or in respect of the author, as when a man makes a law that goes beyond the power committed to him;—or in respect to

the form, as when burdens are imposed unequally on the
community.... The like are acts of violence rather than
laws. Such laws do not bind in conscience.... Secondly,
laws may be unjust through being opposed to the Divine
good, such are the law of tyrants inducing to idolatry....
And laws of this kind must nowise be observed.[101]

The language of Thomas is typically rich with insight. Thomas
tells citizens that rulers who impose unjust laws, inconsistent with
the law of God, are poor rulers promulgating laws not worthy of
our allegiance. Citizens cannot be passive in relation to unjust laws.
Thomas, while urging disobedience, does not recommend the
practice in an absolute sense. Depending on the issue objected to,
the resistance may cause scandal and disquiet in the community
—a price not worth the resistance. In essence Thomas urges the
advocate to find proportionality in the action confronting the unjust law—the proportionality measured by the "injury suffered."[102]
Here again, we witness Thomas' full understanding of how disobedience resides in the public forum. If the action generates too
much turmoil, or the trade off is a greater evil than the justification for the resistance, then prudence dictates a begrudging tolerance of even the unjust law. The word here is tolerance and not
acceptance. He states:

> Wherefore such laws do not bind in conscience, except
> perhaps in order to avoid scandal or disturbance, for
> which cause a man should even yield his right.[103]

Here the moral agent conducts a cost/benefit analysis that depends upon the severity of the injustice. For example the level of
confrontation will inherently be at a more aggressive level when
dealing with the question of abortion, or same sex marriage or
physician assisted suicide, for these dilemmas are so intimately en-
tangled with natural law principles. From another perspective, St.
Thomas will caution the advocate to be less confrontational on
more peripheral matters, such as questions involving gambling, al-
cohol and even drug usage. In both of these cases, St. Thomas displays an uncanny awareness of how the movement of civil disobe-

dience impacts the common good and the collective. Too much protest can undermine the established order since "very grave dissensions"[104] cause such unrest in a community. However, in a tyranny of "excess"[105] the gloves come off for St. Thomas. It is clear that St. Thomas expects the people to rid themselves of the egregious tyrant,

> Furthermore, it seems that to proceed against the cruelty of tyrants is an action to be undertaken … it is not unjust that the king be deposed or have his power restricted … It must not be thought that such a multitude is acting unfaithfully in deposing the tyrant, even though it had previously subject itself to him in perpetuity, because he himself has deserved that the covenant with his subjects should not be kept, since, in ruling the multitude, he did not act faithfully as the office of king demands.[106]

In some respects, St. Thomas posed a radical theory of civil disobedience based on two rationales. First, St. Thomas instructs that unjust laws are not to be recognized, that these enactments cannot bind nor oblige. In the public square citizens can reject human law, can question the legitimacy of a legislative enactment and refuse to observe its language. From any vantage point, this is a very radical posture—that citizens give no recognition to a particular law despite what government says. Secondly, St. Thomas calls for affirmative action in the case of bad law and bad rulers. To not recognize a law requires an affirmation of the law's non-existence. To seek to depose a tyrant, a ruler who crushes the citizenry and burdens the commonwealth with ruthlessness, expressly encourages active political action against the unjust ruler. In this case, we see a continuation of an activist, public mentality whereby the citizen is expected to rise up against the governmental oppression—not in every case to be sure, for St. Thomas types this type of protest as only appropriate in the worst of circumstances. In all of these observations, one recognizes the citizen in action, not in a clandestine fashion but crying out in the forum of public opinion and political reality.

In the realm of Dr. King, public action was part and parcel of civil disobedience. King expressly requires that civil disobedience be done "openly, lovingly and with a willingness to accept the penalty."[107] All of King's means and methods of civil disobedience were carried out in the public square, from the marches to sit-ins, from access blockages to other obstructions, King emphasized both the action chosen and the corresponding reaction. Into the streets King will exhort his followers—tell the entire world of the plight of injustice. In *I've Been to the Mountaintop*, King passionately invites the public to stand tall against injustice.

> Now we are going to march again and we've got to march again, in order to put the issue where it is supposed to be and force everybody to see.… And we've got to say to the nation, we know how it's coming out. For when people get caught up with that which is right and they are willing to sacrifice for it, there is no stopping point short of victory. We aren't going to let any mace stop us. We are masters in our nonviolent movement in disarming police forces. They don't know what to do. I've seen them so often.… By the hundreds we would move out, and Bull Connor would tell them to send the dogs forth, and they did come.… Bull Connor next would say, "Turn the fire hoses on." And as I said to you the other night, Bull Connor didn't know history. He knew a kind of physics that somehow didn't relate to the trans-physics that we knew about.[108]

As Lewis Baldwin observes,

> The whole world was watching as demonstrators were confronted by the hideousness of hatred in its most illogical and virulent forms. When nonviolence was met with violence, observers from all camps, including legal theorists, mainline Christians, and detached jurists, were forced to reconsider the contours of justice in every realm.[109]

As the world watched, as the community experiences first-hand the tactics of civil disobedience as well as the reaction to it, the lesson of injustice unfolds and the quest for a "dignified plea for equality"[110] takes center stage. Being dignified and respectful of even those who despise us is central to King's method. It is the nonviolence that publicly instructs the community and serves as a "substitute against chaos."[111] King found that staying true to the Christian ethic would impress those antagonistic to the cause.

> If we respect those who oppose us, they may achieve a new understanding of the human relations involved.[112]

Just as insightfully, King recognized that institutions entrusted with assuring justice, such as the courts and the churches, would not eliminate injustice without some serious prodding from the resistors. For more than 150 years, decisions from high courts, opinions from clerics and national leaders maintained the status quo of the segregationist mentality. Civil disobedience is the "catalyst"[113] rattling the institutional cages. Civil disobedience challenges the courts, the legislature and government agencies to reconsider a fixed position. While King surely had little objection to peaceful assembly and disobedience on the streets, he gently reminded his followers that redress must simultaneously and continuously be sought in existing institutions, particularly the courts. Public displays are not sufficient without a plan of institutional appeal, but these two approaches are complimentary. In King's magnificent *I Have a Dream*, he realizes that change is coming but too slowly for a frustrated people. To the mass of people on the Washington Mall, he delivers some of this nation's most memorable public oratory.

> We have also come to this hallowed spot to remind America of the fierce urgency of now. There is no time to engage in the luxury of cooling of or to take the tranquilizing drug of gradualism. Now is the time to make real the promises of democracy.[114]

So Martin Luther King—desirous of change, disillusioned about its pace and result, though fully mindful that in time the truth will come out, employs public resistance wherever he can. King does not advocate political revolution but a revolution of the heart and soul of the human person. Bring the truth of the injustice to all open to the truth, and the injustice will melt away. To the universe we make our claim, a universe operating with moral laws—a reflection of the Creator. King passionately argues that the injustice of segregation and inequality, once brought into the open, into the light, will be so obvious that reasonable men and women will seek its ruin. King comments in *Letter from the Birmingham Jail,*

> We merely bring to the surface the hidden tension that is already alive. We bring it out in the open, where it can be seen and dealt with. Like a boil that can never be cured so long as it is covered up but must be opened with all its ugliness to the natural medicines of air and light, injustice must be exposed. With all the tension its exposure creates, to the light of human conscience and the air of national opinion before it can be cured.[115]

Finally, the purest form of civil disobedience engages suffering. Civil disobedience is not supposed to be without ramifications and in fact, the action, in order to have any substantive value, must garner a negative cost to the actor. The true advocate of civil disobedience expects to be arrested and prosecuted, realizes that there might be financial costs to the disobedience and knows that social and cultural alienation might take place. In *Letter from Birmingham Jail,* Dr. King characterizes suffering as essential for self-purification,

> We were not unmindful of the difficulties involved. So we decided to go through a process of self-purification. We started having workshops on nonviolence and repeatedly asked ourselves the questions: Are you able to accept blows without retaliating? Are you able to endure the ordeals of jail?[116]

Suffering and negative consequence are an integral part of the civil disobedience package since "it aroused the conscience of the community over its injustice."[117] Dr. King was fully aware of the price many of his companions paid for the civil disobedience, especially clergy who "have been dismissed from their churches, have lost support of their bishops and fellow ministers."[118] While King was the clear leader of the Civil Rights Movements of his era, he was not unaware that a movement was a body of individuals joined in a common cause. His movement would have not existed without extraordinary personal sacrifice by so many. In *I Have a Dream* he pays tribute the significant costs of disobedience,

> I am not unmindful that some of you have come here out of great trials and tribulations. Some of you have come fresh from narrow jail cells. Some of you have come from areas where your quest for freedom left you battered by the storms of persecution and staggered by the winds of police brutality. You have been the veterans of creative suffering. Continue to work with the faith that unearned suffering is redemptive.[119]

Suffering can be liberating and rewarding when engaged in a just cause. And the protester should not affirmatively seek to avoid the punishment because the punishment is part of the education of the public at large. By accepting the punishment, the party who disobeys is not an anarchist or a revolutionary, but is a good citizen who, "like Socrates, seeks to serve the higher good of the country which gave him or her birth."[120]

For St. Thomas, a theory of non-observance and non-recognition foretells consequence at every level. Just as in King's world, the alienation, loss of privilege and position, prison and incarceration, mental suffering, will potentially accompany the actor's choice. Suffering follows every Christian as he or she lives out their time in the temporal sphere. Suffering, a reflection and participation with the passion of Jesus Christ, who saves us by his suffering, cannot be avoided in the life of a Christian. Instead, suffering should be embraced St. Thomas holds.

> Christ died but once for our sins, therefore a man cannot a second time be likened unto Christ's death by the sacrament of Baptism. Hence it is necessary for those who sin after Baptism be likened unto Christ suffering some form of punishment or suffering which they endure in their own person.... [121]

For the Christian moral agent, choice in moral action, whether it be related to civil rights or equality, human dignity and the preservation of life, appears one dimensional. The rigidity of choice in matters of the natural law, by way of illustration, comes about because the questions are unchangeable, perennial tenets. That the natural law desires us to seek the good, to preserve our life and those of our neighbor, to believe in God, marry and procreate children, are the commandments of the natural law in a nutshell. Anything which assaults these self-evident principles, any law which acts contrarily to the purpose of these propositions, should not be obeyed. Because of these bedrock principles, the resistors are bound to suffer, to be alienated, marginalized, mocked and humiliated. The price one pays to be faithful to justice and law in its truest sense is always high.

St. Thomas is forever sensitive to the fine line between anarchy and righteous civil disobedience. He realizes that individual conscience alone will falter in any assessment of just or unjust laws because the analysis involves more than the preferences of individuals. Of course, Thomas wishes the citizenry to obey and render to Caesar what he is due since "the order of justice requires that subjects obey their superiors, else the stability of human affairs would cease."[122] Despite this general proclamation, St. Thomas does not serve up blind obedience and he fully recognizes that there is a place where disobedience, with all of its punishing consequences, is the better thing to do, for "sometimes the things commanded by a superior are against God. Therefore superiors are not to be obeyed in all things."[123] Herein lays the central dilemma for the human agent about to embark with civil disobedience in mind. How can one be sure that the confrontation be just? When is it permissible to stand fast and reject a human promulgation? How can we be so certain that the human law needs our resistance? St. Thomas provides another rule and measure regarding these complex questions although it requires the recognition that man is composed of material and spiritual parts. So often, modernity forgets about the latter—seeing all things in light of the temporal. If the temporal alone be our slide rule, it will be impossible to ever answer the questions posed above. If we gaze at the heavens, for just a little, we can discover an objective moral order descending from God. Thus, we can conclude, as Thomas puts it,

> Man is bound to obey secular princes in so far as this is required by the order of justice. Wherefore if the prince's authority is not just but usurped, or if he commands what is unjust, his subjects are not bound to obey him ...[124]

CHAPTER 3

Civil Disobedience
and the Christian Conscience

Introduction

The foundation for civil disobedience, in the world of both King and Aquinas, is spiritual. Humanism, in and of itself, cannot provide the justification for civil disobedience. If one seeks to assert a right are these rights natural and "where do they come from? How do we know of them and how do we justify them?"[1] Throughout their legal analysis, they will both posit a higher law jurisprudence that courses its way back to the Creator. In Aquinas we shall witness a systematic, hierarchical construct that commences with the eternal law, God himself, who implants natural laws within his rational creatures, reveals his word in the New and Old Testaments and concludes that human law compliments all of it if consistent.[2] In King, we discern a deeply spiritual, personal legalism, more poetic and Scriptural in design, rooted in Christology and the philosophy of Jesus of Nazareth. King stresses the role of love and charity as remedy to injustice. Dr. King lays out the tradition of Christian civil disobedience in his *Letter from the Birmingham Jail,*

> Whenever the early Christians entered a town the power structure got disturbed and immediately sought to convict them for being "disturbers of the peace" and "outside agitators." But they went on with the conviction that they were "a colony of heaven," and had to obey God rather than man. They were small in number but big in commitment. They were too God-intoxicated to be "astronomically intimidated."[3]

61

So powerful was their example that spectators become converts to this new religion and way of life.

From either school comes the recognition that law cannot exclusively tend to the "secularistic and materialistic,"[4] but higher values—the "highest good of man is his happiness"[5] which culminates in God.

Civil Disobedience and Christian Philosophy

From either perspective, King and Aquinas held firm to Christian ethics as each developed a philosophy of civil disobedience. Neither solely relied on the empty promise of humanism, legal formalism or other theory of secular rights.[6] Christianity was adopted as a matter of habit in the time of St. Thomas and it would have been difficult to conceive any evaluation of moral action being devoid of Christian influence. Even so, St. Thomas is a unique figure who elevates the primacy of reason in theological and philosophical pursuits. In other words, faith and revelation are things of the intellect just as much, or even more, as any other science might be. To Thomas, faith and knowledge are partners in the search for the true. As Dr. King remarks about St. Thomas,

> Thomas Aquinas is probably the first theologian to systematically state the relationship between reason and revelation.... Thomas held that many important doctrines can be demonstrated by reason, e.g. the existence of God and the immortality of the soul.... Thomas makes it clear that because these doctrines are revealed does not mean they are irrational.... So we see in Thomas a harmonious relationship between reason and revelation. Both must exist side by side. They do not conflict; rather they aid each other.[7]

In a sense, it is fair to argue that St. Thomas brings to the table a version of Christian "Rationalism" that encompasses both mind and the soul.[8] Patrick Brennan understands this posture well when he remarks:

> God can speak, according to Thomas, as he is believed to have spoken on Mt. Sinai and at John's baptism of Jesus in the Jordan, for example. Conscience however is not the voice of God but the functioning of (divinely created) human reason.[9]

It is simply impossible to sever God from legal thinking in the world of St. Thomas since "there can be no supreme, ultimate basis for any mandate except the Creator, God, the first unmoved mover, the first uncaused cause, the absolutely necessary being, all-perfect and supreme intelligence."[10] Add to this the intellectual and theological leanings of Aquinas, and it would be impossible to discover an irreligious or amoral posture on the subject.

During the turbulent time of Dr. King, the reliance on spiritual or moral rationales is by no means self-evident. That Dr. King had a myriad of paths towards resistance is well documented.[11] Considering the alternatives of violent action, revolutionary tactics and separatism, King concluded, as did Gandhi, that passive resistance would scream loudly and trigger the most favorable reaction[12] and that comparatively, it was "power" like no other.[13] King is enthralled by Jesus of Nazareth whom King sees as the "model for life an inspiration for life,"[14] as well as a "rebel against the established order."[15] King chose from an extensive menu of options as he devised his plan of action for social change. For example, nothing precluded his choice of violent action, the assertion of might and power by any means in place of non-violence. Nor was there any inherent restriction on whether King chose hatred and ill will as his credo—directed squarely at those institutions and individuals responsible for institutionalized slavery and racism. Surely, King could have identified a plethora of targets to hate and despise. Just as plausible would be King's aggressive choice of separatism and alienation from the white race by urging his followers to see white citizens as enemies to be either overthrown or shunned. He had a multitude of choices most of which promoted or fed upon the anger and anguish of a community long suffering. King could have readily tapped into the negative and darkest side of the problem so to speak. Yet, King chose the path of love and charity, the road of redemption and forgiveness and urged his followers to disobey with the passion of righteousness and justice. Most take for granted this choice. King's theory of civil disobedience was rooted in more than opposition to a particular law but rather embedded in the Christian ideal of love. Dr. King appreciates the range of choices but the necessity of Christian love as his grounding when he remarks,

> Justice is what love sounds like when it speaks in public. Civic piety is love's public language, equality is tone of voice and freedom its constant pitch.[16]

King knows only too well the vacuousness of humanism untethered to the God of Abraham. King finds nothing all that compelling about humanism since this "particular sort of optimism has been discredited by the brutal logic of events."[17] In this extraordinary time of tumult and revolt, with pressure from any and every quarter, King chose the path of peaceful non-violence. As he remarks:

> As seen in the life and teaching of Jesus, humanity remains conscious of its humble dependence upon God, as the source of all being and all goodness. "There is none good save one, even God.[18]

The Role of Christian Love in Civil Disobedience

In the works of King and Aquinas, there is little question that their jurisprudence is heavily influenced by the principles of Christian charity. King indicated many times that he would rather love "than hate" urging sisters and brothers that "love is the only way."[19] Love, as Jesus would have it, is a tough road in a world of injustice. King tells us that Jesus commands that we love our enemies, for "love is understanding, redemptive goodwill for all men, so that you love everybody, because God loves them."[20] In this sense,

3 · CIVIL DISOBEDIENCE AND THE CHRISTIAN CONSCIENCE   65

King fully appreciates not only the intricacies of civil society and
its democratic mechanics but the essential role of the human person in that society. Put another way, King recognizes that individual dignity, tethered to a creative and loving God, is what shores
up his decision-making in the matter of resistance. King adopts
the "Social Gospel" as a blueprint for life and living with Christ as
its perfect model.[21] Even the worst of the worst, deserve love for
every creature has "an element of goodness that he can never
slough off"[22] since the human agent is fashioned by God. In King's
Sermon, *The American Dream*, he publishes a blueprint for civil
disobedience as espoused by his predecessor Aquinas and earlier
Augustine.

> We need not hate; we need not use violence. We can stand
> up before our most violent opponent and say: We will
> match your capacity to inflict suffering by our capacity to
> endure suffering. We will meet your physical force with
> soul force. Do to us what you will and we will still love
> you. We cannot in good conscience obey your unjust laws,
> because non-cooperation with evil is as much a moral ob-
> ligation as is cooperation with good ... [23]

Love is the other path for the resistor. Hate burdens and shack-
les the human person and gets in the way of true reform. King
proclaims that there is "power" in love unlike all other compar-
isons.[24] Indeed in King's world, nonviolent resistance will be based
upon the "principle of love."[25] In *The American Dream*, he could
not advocate for love with more fervor,

> Oh yes, love is the way. Love is the only absolute. More
> and more I see this. I've seen too much hate to want to
> hate myself; hate is too great a burden to bear. I've seen it
> on the faces of too many sheriffs in the South—I've seen
> hate. In the faces and even the walk of too many Klans-
> men of the South, I've seen hate. Hate distorts the per-
> sonality. Hate does something to the soul that causes one
> to lose objectivity. The man who hates can't think
> straight.[26]

King distinguishes two types of love: *eros* or aesthetic, that which deals with beauty; *agape*—the non-physical love, the love friendship, mother to child, human person to God. It is the latter, "agape" love that drives his enterprise. King indicates.

> *Agape* is understanding, creative, redemptive good will for all men. Biblical theologians would say it is the love of God working in the minds of men. It is an overflowing love which seeks nothing in return. And when you come to love on this level you begin to love men not because they are likeable, not because they do things that attract us, but because God loves them and here we love the person who does the evil deed while hating the deed that the person does. It is the type of love that stands at the center of the movement that we are trying to carry on in the Southland—*agape*.[27]

Contrary to its imagery, love is also formidable power according to King. Not the power of military and political might, but as an agent for change. There is no more efficacious change medium than love. Love can "implement the demands of ... justice."[28] Power exercises without love and is "reckless and abusive."[29]

St. Thomas is no less passionate about the role and place of Christian love and charity in his legal theory. In Christ is the "first truth which illuminates and teaches man inwardly."[30] It is in the order of things that human kind loves both God and their neighbor—it is how things must be in God's rational plan. As Thomas notes in his *Summa Contra Gentiles*:

> Again, whoever loves a person must, as a consequence, also love those loved by that person and those related to him. Now, men are loved by God, for He has prearranged for them, as an ultimate end, the enjoyment of Himself. Therefore, it should be that, as a person becomes a love of God, he also becomes a lover of his neighbor.[31]

For the Christian, the adoption and maintenance of love as the chief catalyst in human action is no easy task. Aquinas appreciates the labor it takes to unreservedly live in charity, to understand law in the larger sense in regard to individual neighbor and the collective at large, and to see how any notions of rights and correlating justice need depend on a theory of love. In the *Summa Contra Gentiles*, St. Thomas poetically poses the dilemma for those who choose love over other motivators in human action.

> In fact, this is accomplished by man's love of God and his neighbor, for he who loves a person gives him his due spontaneously and joyfully, and he even adds something in excess of liberality. So the complete fulfillment of the law depends on love, according to the text of the Apostle: "Love is the fulfilling of the law" (Rom. 3:10). And the Lord says that "on these two commandments," that is, love of God and of neighbor, "dependeth the whole law" (Matt. 22:40).[32]

Those who act out of hate rather than charity can neither get along with self nor reside peacefully in a community. The racist hates; the racist holds tightly onto the passions at the expense of reason and the racist, in the final analysis hates oneself. In his assessment of Aristotelian friendship, Aquinas discerns how a life without Christian charity leads to an immeasurable void.

> First, as to living together, for the wicked cannot live with themselves, but seek others with whom to live, speaking and acting with them according to external words and acts. This they do as soon as they think of themselves they remember the many great and wicked things they have committed in the past and presume they will do the same in the future, which is painful to them. But when they are with other men, pouring themselves out in external things, they forget their evils. Thus, because they have nothing in themselves worthy of love, they do nothing friendly towards themselves.[33]

Aquinas fully appreciates the corrosive impact of hate over love for hate is a "spiritual darkness."[34]

In Christian love, the agent of civil disobedience finds solace and contentment in the choice. Love "directs all the acts of the other virtues"[35] giving "sustenance and nourishment"[36] to all human action.

Divine Underpinnings in Civil Disobedience

According to King and Aquinas, a legal system stripped of its divine underpinnings, shed of its obligation to the higher law of God, fails to bind any man, any citizen in the commonwealth. In Aquinas there is a metaphysical dignity to the human person, a root foundation for natural, undeniable and inalienable rights. The dignity of the human person "arises in at least three ways: from his origin (created directly by God), his end (made for God), and his inherent dignity possessed by every human person."[37] All law inevitably discovers its legitimacy by discovering the Creator who creates the human player. Nothing man constructs can rise to a level that justifies dignity of any sort and "betrays us into imagining these rights and obligations as realities existing apart from the law...."[38] Aquinas emphatically ties the divine to human operations since we are the rational byproducts of a perfect God. He remarks,

> Human law has the nature of law in so far as it partakes of right reason; and it is clear that, in this respect, it is derived from the eternal law. But in so far as it deviates from reason, it is called an unjust law, and has the nature, not of law but of violence.[39]

Aquinas construes law, and the rights that emanate there from, as nothing more or less than an imprint from the Creator—an orderly set of inclinations, predispositions and predilections that make Homo Sapiens function in accordance with our proper ends. Only man is capable of this sort of imprint since as a rational creature "it is appropriate that law {to} be given men by God."[40] Natural law is embedded in the mind of man infused as an "imprint on us of the Divine light."[41] As such, any notion of a legal right inevitably weaves its way back to the metaphysical rather than the temporal. True rights must rest on the higher plane versus the gritty earth of practical reality. Any basis for the advocacy of a human right, whether it be desegregation or human equality cannot solely be gauged from human affairs. These rights are "extra- and supra-legal. Rights derive directly from God or Nature, from the ultimate structure of things—and they belong to man as part of his intrinsic nature, as much as his body, his mind and his various powers."[42] In short, a theory of civil disobedience finds no solace in an individual preference or opinion but instead need rest in something universally dependable. Nothing human escapes the fleeting nature of things. Nothing human, in and of itself, can ever provide the necessary justification. The same can be said of the nationalist clamor since these movements have short life spans as the Third Reich so keenly proves. Man and country alone do not deliver the support for any theory of civil disobedience. Law cannot rest on this sort of shaky frame since "it cannot be legitimately legalized if it be contrary to the moral law."[43] Casting God aside seems easy in a culture bent on secularism and materialism—for God, in a way, gets in the way of what people want to do in a wrongful sense.

Dr. King reaches an identical conclusion about the emptiness of a strictly secular legal system and recognizes that unjust laws are inconsistent in the eye and mind of a perfect God. Segregation laws, laws that promote inequality and injustice cannot square with the moral law. The racist treads "in the confused waters of secularism."[44] In the final analysis, King contends:

> The highest court of justice is in the heart of man when he is inspired by the teaching of Christ. Rather than being the judge, Christ is the light in which we pass judgment on ourselves. The truth is that every day our deeds and words, our silence and speech, are building character. Any day that reveals this fact is a day of judgment.[45]

In the larger sense, King's notion of law and justice, as that of Aquinas, cannot be severed from the divine. No matter how unjust the present may be, there is another dimension, a spiritual one where God resides—"a Life beyond life."[46] The Civil Rights Movement need elevate the human person although elevation is merely a pronouncement or promulgation but the undeniable recognition that rights emerge and arise from God and His Son Jesus Christ. In fact, King praises modern Neo-Thomism as an antidote to injustice by noting that its tenets "preserve the dignity of man and rescue the valuable elements in humanistic culture by incorporating them in a new Christian civilization."[47] King argues eloquently in *Strength to Love*,

> Man, for Jesus, is not mere flotsam and jetsam in the river of life, but he is a child of God. It is not unreasonable to assume that God, whose creative activity is expressed in an awareness of a sparrow's fall and the numbers of hairs on a man's head, excludes from his encompassing love the life of man itself?[48]

Hence, King cannot sever his call to civil disobedience from the higher power of his Creator. To resist unjust human laws will call upon the resistor to metaphysically justify the action. As King remarked, "Freedom requires metaphysical otherness."[49] Without God as center of the struggle, King would claim, "all our efforts turn to ashes and our sunrises into the darkest nights."[50]

Aquinas long held the same for an unjust law deserves no recognition, nor can it bind or oblige in anyway if severed from the author of the eternal law, nor should Christians stand by and allow its imposition to injure or harm others. Aquinas notes very clearly:

> Accordingly all that is in things created by God, whether it be contingent or necessary, is subject to the eternal law: while things pertaining to Divine Nature or Essence are not subject to the eternal law, but are the eternal law itself.[51]

This recognition that the spiritual guides the lawmaker and the citizen subject to them, rests centrally in the legal ethic of St. Thomas. The commands of men must always be rooted in Christian charity so "any commandment to do something would be pointless if doing it were not more characteristic of charity than not doing it."[52]

For both Aquinas and King, the citizen is urged to not only resist evil but to stamp it out and to do so by employing a Christ centered theology. To be a true Christian surely has political and economic consequences. If the law of the Gospel takes center stage for the human agent, it urges that player to act in distinct and non-negotiable ways. Civil disobedience does not arise because of conflicting viewpoints, or mere argument and disagreement. Civil disobedience implies a dependency on a higher ethic that justifies the disobedience. Any other form of civil disobedience will fall on its own insufficiency. Justifiable civil disobedience contemplates the right, "summum bonum" and the plan of the Creative God. Surely the mandate of laws, of whatever ilk, cannot and do not inherently assure the right of any particular action. Aquinas had an exceptionally keen understanding of why the citizen should not obey mindlessly—and that understanding fully recognized the inherent inadequacy of some human promulgation. Obedience for what end, for what purpose, to what aim, would always concern St. Thomas. For example, when speaking of a vow or a promise, St. Thomas illustrates the meaninglessness of a vow in the human context alone. Why should one promise at all? He edifies:

> Before you made yourself liable under a vow, you were free to remain at a lower level, though we should not applaud a freedom which means that we are not obliged to do something which it is profitable to do....But now your promise is lodged with God.... but now if, God forbid, you break that pledge you have given to God, you will be as much more wretched as you would blessed if you keep it.[53]

Aquinas assumes that a vow had to be anchored in a higher order, a view that what we tell others is true—not because we say it so, but because we must communicate with truth. A secular, sectarian system of law and its enforcement lacks moral credibility and its corresponding state or governmental structure will be equally deficient. It is the natural law principles espoused by Aquinas that give meaning and substance to any claims of rights and "provides the best defense against legal tyranny."[54] And truth sits above and beyond the temporal sphere as does any essential meaning of the term law. For King, the citizenry, bogged down with material and strictly secular concerns, will lose the true and bona fide rationalization for civil disobedience. In addition, a citizenry stripped of its moral moorings will become complacent and generally unconcerned about the injustice of segregation or anything else for that matter. With unbridled passion, King recognized that his cause was beyond the context of race, creed or color but something borne out of perennial truth and certitude. His cause, while surely aimed at the injustice heaped upon a segregated class, constituted an even higher calling. That calling embodied all human beings regardless of ethnicity or other criteria. King appealed to his white brethren to see the movement as equally applicable to them as his constituency—to "seek justice for both himself and the white man."[55] Both King and Aquinas discern the critical and undeniable role of Christian Ethics as rationalization for a particular action. King urges his followers to never forget this interplay,

> I am impelled to write you concerning the responsibilities laid upon you to live as Christians in the midst of an un-Christian world. That is what I had to do. That is what every Christian has to do. But I understand that there are many Christians in America that give their ultimate allegiance to man-made systems and customs. They are afraid to be different.[56]

For King, a resistance rooted in Christian love is far preferable than one grounded in hate and violence. To be a Christian demands that we suffer the insults and affronts with both charity and mercy towards those inflicting these harms. King urges his followers to heed the *modus operandi* of the Christian—exhorting this path of love over all other remedies.

> We don't have to argue with anybody. We don't have to curse and go around acting bad with our words. We don't need any bricks and bottles, we don't need any Molotov cocktails, we just need to go around to these stores, and to these massive industries in our country and say, "God sent us by here, to say that you're not treating his children right. And we've come by here to ask you to make the first item on your agenda—fair treatment, where God's children are concerned."[57]

In the world of King and Aquinas, the material and the secular should be second fiddle to higher notions of the divine. This is one of King's better insights—that segregation and slavery find a place outside of the divine, that the secular and the material can just about justify anything that men and women undertake and that morality has been vanquished by other cravings, whether it be political or economic. King chides modern man who has "allowed the material means by which you live to outdistance the spiritual ends for which you live."[58] Historic truth and the perennial morality that guides human action has been replaced with a passion for science—a genius in and of science while dumbing down any semblance of morality.[59] Aquinas sees this dilemma in a similar way—as men lust for things of the material world they lose sight of the tried and true, the good and the beautiful. Aquinas can only find truth in God—that anchor for human action. Wealth, honors, bodily pleasure and power do not deliver dependable happiness nor do these attainments assure an ethic worth measuring. "God who is goodness itself is the only object that can exhaust the formally under which we desire and act. Perfect happiness for man thus resides in loving union with goodness itself, God."[60] For Aquinas, it is God alone, as source of truth and happiness, which could be relied upon. He notes,

> Happiness is the attainment of the Perfect Good. Whoever, therefore, is capable of the Perfect Good can attain happiness. Now, that man is capable of the Perfect Good is proved both because his intellect can apprehend the universal and perfect good, and because his will can desire it. And therefore man can attain Happiness—This can be proved again from the fact that man is capable of seeing God.[61]

The Compatibility of Non-Violence and Christian Tradition

Non-violence as a methodology sits most comfortably in the chamber of Christianity. Indeed if we heed the exhortation of Jesus to "turn the other cheek," in an ideal sense, non-violence would be the sole means of resistance in matters of injustice. Of course this conclusion is very simplistic since Christian tradition clearly permits self-defense and the use of force in a just war.[62] Aquinas is quite plain on the legitimacy of such action and shows no hesitation in arguing the legality of physical force in self-defense since,

> One's intention is to save one's life, is not unlawful, seeing that it is natural to everything to keep itself in being, as far as possible.... It is not unlawful for a man to intend killing a man in self-defense....[63]

Even so, the primacy of love and forgiveness are undeniable components of Christian action. And in a very curious way, the impact of the Judeo-Christian tradition on the American experience appears more imbedded in the national psyche than other nation states. In fact, Dr. King frequently connected two dots—the Christian and the Constitution. James Hanigan tackles this issue,

> Law, as we have been using the term here, meant to King concretely the Constitution of the United States, a document which to his mind was fully in accord with his understanding of Christianity.[64]

Dr. King, as leader of movement for change, fully understood that both his followers and his critics were, at times, impatient with his peaceful methods. Two centuries of injustice needed a faster means of correction than the slow, deliberate methods of non-violence he urged on his followers. King labeled these frustrations as being borne from "deferred dreams."[65] Other sectors in the movement for change found this plodding and penchant to love thy enemies a sure method for little or no change. Throughout his advocacy, King never loses sight of his Christian obligation. When compared to all the other alternatives to action, the choice of non-violence seems most appropriate.

Some might argue that inaction be the best course. This school of letting sleeping dogs lie avoids confrontation at all costs and hopes that things get better over time, or that things are so structurally corrupt that change is an impossibility. Inactivity is inconsistent with the Christian tradition for a Christian must affirma-tively act in cases of injustice. Aquinas exhorts the Christian moral agent to act.[66] King labels this mentality as "nihilistic"[67] and a "die-hard mentality that sought to shut all windows and doors against the winds of change" which "carries the seeds of its own doom."[68]

Others claim that violence produces quick results and shakes the cobwebs out of existing institutions in order that change might happen. King struggled with diverse antagonists on this topic, from radical Black extremists to the passion of the Black Power ad-vocates; he valiantly cajoled these alternative groups to consider the immorality of their approach while recognizing the wisdom of non-violence. King fully discerns the dilemma of violence as *modus operandi* when rejecting the tactics of Black Power. If there be any revolution at all, it must be interiorly or as he put it, a "rev-olution of values."[69] King could never advocate violence for the means sullies the end. He notes,

> Over the last few years I have consistently preached that nonviolence demands that the means we use must be as pure as the ends we seek. So I have tried to make it clear that it is wrong to use immoral means to attain moral ends.[70]
> It is not the violence of the sword or stone that will re-caste and reshape the world, but the liberation that only comes from Christian love and the Gospel values of Jesus Christ. Beyond the pragmatic invalidity of violence is its inability to appeal to conscience. Some Black Power ad-vocates consider an appeal to conscience irrelevant. A Black Power exponent said to me, not long ago: "To hell with conscience and morality. We want power." But power and morality must go together, implementing, fulfilling and ennobling each other. In this question for power I cannot by pass the concern for morality.[71]

When his critics became exacerbated at this tolerance and pa-tience with those who inflicted insult, King would remind them that the Christian must carry a Cross, must bear burdens and live with forgiveness in one's heart. The alternative to this is destruction. King mentions in a host of places the corrosive power of hatred.

> Through violence you may murder the hater, but you do
> not murder hate. In fact, violence merely increases hate.
> So it goes. Returning violence for violence multiplies vi-
> olence, adding deeper darkness to a night already devoid
> of stars.[72]

For the Christian, the remedy of non-violence fits like a glove because it creates a "beloved community"[73] and awakens "a sense of shame within the oppressor but the end is reconciliation, the end is redemption."[74] Inaction or violent action will lead to a chaos, an abyss in which the dignity of man will long be lost. Communism and Fascism have proven this thesis. No one knows this better than Martin Luther King, Jr. With all the criticisms and pressures exerted upon him; with all the competing approaches to change and revolution, he stood steadfast, confident in his mission but even surer of his methods. In the end, it comes down to two choices: *nonviolent cooperation* or *violent coannihilation*.[75]

CHAPTER 4

The Principle of Non-Recognition

Introduction

The power of any law depends on a variety of factors, none more contemporary than promulgation. Positivism, the predominant legal theory of modernity, holds that the efficacy of any law depends first and foremost on its enactment. A law is a law because it is. Positivism seeks no other territory, and as such, questions as to its validity and ethic, rarely go beyond the text itself. It is rare for a positivist to really object to any law on jurisprudential grounds although it is common to challenge its constitutionality or legislative regularity. There is nothing very radical about this school except its narrow vision about law and its definition. St. Thomas and Dr. King value law in a more grandiose way—defining in universal and cosmological grounds. As a result, there will be times when the printed law will not mean much in their respective worlds. Succinctly, both of them will reach a conclusion, in select cases, that a law, despite its promulgation, lacks the qualities of a law.

Law That Cannot Bind

If there is any thread shared by both Aquinas and King, it is the view that immoral and unjust laws and promulgations cannot oblige or bind the human agent. Whether a law has any binding effect will remain the seminal question for Dr. King throughout his life. Just as Thomas deduced, laws oblige only in certain cases —laws bind when, and only when, they are instruments of justice and truth.[1] In the world of King and Aquinas we discern a full recognition that human law can only go so far, and in the final analysis, the problems of injustice and inhumanity are fundamentally resolved by "a willingness of men to obey the unenforceable."[2] St. Thomas explicitly describes how a law, even though on the books, is really not a law but something else.

A tyrannical law, through not being according to reason, is not a law absolutely speaking, but rather a perversion of law; and yet in so far as it is something in the nature of a law, it aims at the citizens being good.[3]

How men justify racism and inequality cannot be described as noble. And at times, the legal landscape that King encountered was utterly distressing and marked "by a temptation to despair because it is clear now how deep and systematic are the evils it confronts."[4] Human laws are what subjected him to a myriad of indignities. Human laws promoting and enforcing segregation, King argues have, "caused the darkness."[5] Human law provides both remedy and curse in the world of Dr. King, but before he employs the promulgations of man, he will adhere to a Thomistic vision of law. It is his anchor in a sea of social turbulence.

Indeed both urge that we do all in our power to caste out the injustice and the unjust ruler. We are, Aquinas holds, compelled to not only disobey an unjust law but also remove the ruler who promulgates the injustice. Quite radically, St. Thomas relates:

Nor would it be a violation of fidelity at all, according to the opinion of many, to frustrate the wickedness of tyrants by any means whatsoever.[6]

For Thomas, non-recognition can be best characterized as a duty and obligation of the citizen. One resists the unjust ruler not only because of the injustice thrust upon the citizenry but also because the unjust ruler acts against the Godhead of creation. Indeed resistance can be justified by the desire to restore tranquility to a community, though more compellingly because every injustice insults God. St. Thomas urges the citizen to obey when the promulgation is worthy of adherence and to resist when the law contradicts the Divine. In his assessment of obedience, St. Thomas cannot be plainer:

> It is necessary to obey God rather than human beings. And sometimes the commands of the superior are contrary to God. Therefore superiors are not to be obeyed in everything.[7]

Civil law cannot undermine the human conscience, nor force the actor to disregard fundamental truths. Civil law cannot "take the place of conscience or dictate norms concerning things which are outside its competence...."[8] On its face, the finding is quite radical. In this scenario, the proponent argues that even though a law has been promulgated, it cannot bind us in any sense, and therefore cannot compel obedience. Aquinas evaluates whether all law binds in any sense, and he keenly distinguishes between those types of law that do and those that cannot.[9] And if this be so, may a citizen justifiably refuse to adhere to the content and tenets of said law, and even more particularly, is that same citizen, obliged to resist that law and work to its undoing?[10] Aquinas is quite distrustful of the lawmaker who promulgates bad or unjust laws—comparing the legislator as nothing better than a "raging beast" that citizens should avoid at all costs.[11] This inability to bind a citizen, that is to oblige obedience thereto, comes to depend on whether the law is a just one or not. Just laws demand our allegiance, while unjust laws cannot bind us. Obedience cannot be absolute in the legal context for either King or Aquinas. St. Thomas urges the moral agent to think ethically before compliance. He states:

> So we can distinguish three types of obedience: one which is sufficient for salvation, which obeys in those things in which it is strictly bound; one which is perfect and obeys in everything that is not unlawful, and one which is indiscriminating and foolish, which obeys in even things that are unlawful.[12]

Of course, Aquinas is well aware that tyrants and evil rulers throughout history may have the temporal power to impose the unjust law on the citizenry, but this imposition will not stand the test of time. As St. Thomas holds:

> This is very clear, too, if we consider the means by which a tyrannical government is upheld. It is not upheld by love, since there is little or no bond of friendship between the subject multitude and the tyrant.... Those who are kept down by fear will rise against their rulers if the opportunity ever occurs when they can hope to do it with impunity, and they will rebel against their rulers all the more furiously the more they have been kept in subjection against their will by fear alone, just as water confined under pressure flows with greater impetus when it finds an outlet. That very fear itself is not without danger because many become desperate from excessive fear, and despair of safety impels a man boldly to dare anything. Therefore the government of a tyrant cannot be of long duration.[13]

The Measure of Unjust Laws

Exactly how does one conclude that a law needs no recognition? For both St. Thomas and Dr. King, unjust laws fail on various fronts and are subject to diverse tests. The critical issue is this: What measure or criteria prompts a finding of injustice in law? The trick is finding a measure—some yardstick that instructs on when a law is good or not. Cicero employed nature as his measure.[14] St. Thomas manifests a strong Ciceronian tendency in his *Summa Contra Gentiles*. In responding to a query on the impact and effect of promulgation alone, St. Thomas makes plain that promulgation may be at odds with what is right and therefore lack the essential qualities of a law. St. Thomas holds:

> Again, men receive from divine providence a natural capacity for rational judgment, as a principle for their proper operations. Now, natural principles are ordered to natural results. So, there are certain operations that are

naturally suitable for man, and they are right in themselves not merely because they are prescribed by law.[15]

Nature provides instruction, according to Aquinas "for whatever is in accord with nature is best, for in all things nature does
what is best."[16]

St. Thomas even more clearly adopts the Aristotelian virtue theory whereby the suitability of a law will depend on its capacity to
habituate citizens to virtue.[17] Aside from the individual understanding relative to virtue, Aquinas ties in the collective, the common good as an endgame for all law. Any law which does not advance the general welfare of the citizenry, tending the citizenry to
goodness, suffers definitionally. St. Thomas holds:

> Consequently the law must needs regard principally the re-
> lationship to happiness. Moreover, since every part is or-
> dained to the whole, as imperfect to perfect; and since one
> man is a part of the perfect community, the law must needs
> regard properly the relationship to universal happiness.[18]

Aquinas builds on both schools, that of Aristotelian virtue and
Ciceronian nature, and then proposes a natural law model
whereby the human agent has impressed into his very essence, embedded into his very being and psyche, certain undeniable first
principles. These natural law impressions, the "truth of our conclusions"—those that are discovered and concluded by "men and
women of different cultures that have arrived at over the centuries,"[19] provide another very dependable measure. A human law
compatible with the natural law is surely worthy of our allegiance.

King clearly depends on this Thomistic construct—that laws,
unjust in design, need not be recognized. The conclusion results
from an evaluation as to whether the law in question is consistent
or antagonistic to the natural law.[20] The first principles of the natural law are self-evident—that we seek good, wish to live in a social community, pine for children and by implication desire het-
erosexual means to propagate, self-preservation and believe in
God. There is nothing all that amazing in these conclusions,
Aquinas tells us, since this is how human beings act. If a law ad-

vances these predispositions and predilections, it is good law. If it is deleterious to these inclinations, it is unjust.[21] Hence abortion laws which permit the act, are in direct contravention to the natural law principle of self preservation. As is suicide and euthanasia. In this sense, Aquinas looks to our nature, just as early Roman and Greek thinkers had done, using it as a benchmark for human conduct. This portrayal, however, is woefully unsophisticated, for St. Thomas erects an unrivaled natural law model which encompasses the imprint of the Creator. There are not many rules to the imprint, but these first principles are undeniable and non-negotiable. John Finnis argues that the natural law theory of Aquinas boils down to seven basic goods—*knowledge of truth, life and health, play, aesthetic experience, friendship, practical reasonableness and religion.*[22] There is much disagreement about whether this measure works.[23]

Any law operating in opposition to these fundamental principles lacks the force and power of law. Law, in the positive sense, cannot bind or oblige unless it directs species "to its proper end."[24] Unjust laws cannot bind, cannot oblige and cannot compel a citizen to adherence. Aquinas, employing the Augustinian precept, tells us that an "unjust law is not a law at all."[25] In fact, Aquinas argues that a law which is unjust does "violence"[26] to any notion of what a law is or should be. Some commentators use even harsher descriptions like "reign of terror"[27] as law makers enact unjust laws. King likes to label these laws as unenforceable while Aquinas types them as a sort of legal nihilism. Either approach leads in the same direction. King argues:

> But unenforceable obligations are beyond the reach of the laws of society. They concern inner attitudes, expression of compassion which law books cannot regulate and jails cannot rectify. Such obligations are met by a one's commitment to an inner law, a law written on the heart. Man-made laws assure justice, but a higher law produces love.[28]

Just as Aquinas does, King not only refuses to recognize the unjust law, but also concludes that the Christian has an affirmative obligation to undermine and unseat such laws. King holds that the

Christian "owes his ultimate allegiance to God, and if any earthly institution conflicts," it is the duty of every Christian "to take a stand against it."[29] Exactly when that stand should be taken is a less precise question for those laboring as judges, lawyers and other justice officials. On closer inspection, this right to resist does not apply in every scenario, nor would it be an avenue for those who simply disagree on this or that. And in fact questions regarding that right to resist and disobey are not always as black and white as they appear. William Pryor concludes that our governing bodies are often wrong in decision-making, often erect unsound policies and even adopt practices that are contrary to the Judeo-Christian ethic. These negatives alone may not give rise to the ethical resistance as Pryor notes,

> Our moral duty to obey the government, even when we believe its commands are unsound, is for our protection and the common good. We live in a sinful world, as Heaven awaits, and the government exists to punish evil, although imperfectly. The government is God's institution for securing justice in our fallen world until we can enter Heaven through Christ's saving grace.[30]

Hence there are many things that may not be right, but are not the proper subject matter for non-recognition and civil disobedience. Herein is the crux of the matter—that resistance depends on the thing to be resisted. In a more global context, St. Thomas displays conservatism when applying these principles to entire governments. In his assessment of tyrants, and what to do about them, St. Thomas shows a pragmatic streak regarding injustice. Sometimes, disobedience may whip up more injustice due to the reaction of the tyrant. Other times, the tyranny may be less evil or grievous, a "milder tyranny,"[31] thereby making disobedience the less prudential route. Aquinas relays that unless there is an excess of tyranny, it is better to be "reverently subject to our masters, not only to the good and gentle but also the froward."[32]

For Aquinas, the resistance inexorably winds its way back to the fundamental first principles of the natural law. These principles, often labeled, predispositions, inclinations or tendencies, are primordial rules of human operation. Natural laws are first principles of human conduct—those things that are an undeniable part of our makeup—the things that all human beings share; that cannot be blotted out, changed or altered, and that are universal and permanent rules.[33] Laws that are in opposition to these first principles would be laws in need of not only non-recognition but affirmative resistance or non-cooperation. To illustrate, laws legitimizing physician assisted suicide, incest or murder, could not be laws in any sense since these promulgations are directly contrary to the self-preservation principle of the natural law. In other words, there are not many times when the non-recognition concept kicks in but a glance at the natural law will instruct on when and where. In the case of slavery, that is laws that promote the enslavement of a race of people, directly opposes the tenets of the natural law. Such injustices must be actively resisted.

In sum, the duty of resistance depends on the subject matter; the matter of non-recognition will come to depend on the severity of the case in question and whether there is room for rational disagreement.[34]

Civil Disobedience and an Objective Moral Order

If all things are relative, any basis for resistance to a particular law withers. Only an objective moral basis, which is a moral order, built on certitude and universality will work in the context of civil disobedience. By objective one means that the morality is true in all cases; that the morality applies to all persons, nations and circumstances, not man alone as "autonomous arbiter of right and wrong."[35] Contrasted with the relative, the objective moral order seeks the universal, immutable and unchangeable and the perennially timeless criteria. Both St. Thomas and Dr. King advocate an objective moral code, though each approaches the objectivity with differing styles. Aquinas is typically systematic, stressing the hierarchical dynamic of the eternal law descending, though fully interdependent, to the human law. King's emphasis tends to be highly theological, indicative of his deep felt personalism[36] in matters of injustice. In addition, King never addresses objectivity in any one work but his musings are sprinkled throughout his bibliography. What is undeniable is King's castigation of the current passion for relativity in matters of morality when he says:

> The other thing is that we have adopted a sort of a pragmatic test for right and wrong—whatever works is right. If it works, it's alright. Nothing is wrong but that which does not work. If you don't get caught it's right. That's the attitude, isn't it? If it's all right to disobey the Ten Commandments, but just don't disobey the Eleventh, Thou shall not get caught. That's the attitude. That's the prevailing attitude in our culture. No matter what you do, just do it with a bit of finesse.[37]

King labels our universe as "law abiding"—a world that "hinges on moral foundations... and based on moral law."[38] He often makes the comparison that moral law operates identically to physical laws evident in the universe. Arguing like Cicero,[39] King concludes that there is a moral operation in nature and the physical universe. When Cicero states that justice can be found in nature, he foretells the argument that King offers. In *Strength to Love*, one discerns this tendency.

> God walks with us. He has placed within the very structure of this universe certain absolute moral laws. We can neither defy nor break them. If we disobey them, they will break us.[40]

The insight, that the universe is mechanically moral, can only provide optimism as King leads his movement since it is not a condition that is temporary or subject to political whim. The world, in and of itself is moral, a "silent, invisible imperative, akin to the law in the physical world."[41]

In King we discover objectivity rooted in the "good"—not the stuff of personal preference and individual pleasure, but the Platonic and Aristotelian good that leads to human happiness. At the

ultimate end of the human person, God, we find the author of all
that is good and true—caretaker of the objective moral code. This
is a code that operates and inherently attaches itself to the universe.
As King remarks,

> That there is something unfolding in the universe whether
> one speaks of it as a unconscious process, or whether one
> speaks of it as some unmoved mover, or whether some-
> one speaks of it as a personal God. There is something in
> the universe that unfolds for justice and so in Mont-
> gomery we felt somehow that as we struggled we had
> cosmic companionship. And this was one of the things
> that kept the people together, the belief that the universe
> is on the side of justice.[42]

For Aquinas, the justification for disobedience will arise and be
grounded upon the permanent and unflinching first principles of
human operation of the natural law. These tenets are fully discoverable in reason. Every human being can "naturally apprehend as
being odd the five things to which human beings have a natural
inclination: seeking the good, preserving one's own life, preserving the species, living in community with others and knowing the
truth and choosing how to act in accordance with it."[43] Certitude
of knowledge regarding natural law principles is very achievable
according to St. Thomas.

> Consequently, we must say that the natural law, as to gen-
> eral principles, is the same for all, both as to rectitude and
> as to knowledge.[44]

In the subjective domain, the morality will ebb and flow according to preference, whim, power or status, fad or the clamor
of the masses. Patrick Clancy sums up the dilemma cogently,

> Yet, whether its author be ecclesiastical or civil, human
> law bears the stamp of its ancestry.... Civil law is derived
> proximately from Natural Law, while all ecclesiastical law
> can be traced back, proximately either to the Natural Law

or to divine revelation. Otherwise the result is neither human nor law.[45]

A theory of non-recognition, laboring under a subjective thesis, has no sustainability. In Aquinas, the objective moral order finds a home in his theory of natural law—a series, albeit very small, of propositions and predilections in the human person—true in all persons and all cases. The content of the natural law can be summed up in his first principle—to seek and yearn for the good and to avoid evil or harm. Is this not the template of the human person—to grow, to yearn for happiness, to pine for all that is good and shun that which destroys us? Indeed St. Thomas directly links the natural law to virtue. In other words, every principle of the natural law has virtue in its sight.[46]

Mark Edward DeForrest's exceptional commentary on Civil Disobedience captures the clear necessity of moral objectivity,

> This objective moral standard is by its nature universal. It does not change simply because one is in a different country or a different time period. The objective moral standard is the same whether we are in first century Rome, sixteenth century Germany, or twentieth century China. We do not create the moral standard, nor does it shift to accommodate our changing tastes and appetites. Instead of manufacturing moral truth, human beings arrive at grounded moral knowledge through active participation in and recognition of the objective moral order that has always existed.[47]

For Aquinas, this is an objective fact—that human beings seek the good. Under this grander principle, Aquinas proposes a few others that flesh out the objective principles discoverable in the natural law:

* Self Preservation and the Maintenance of Life
* Family as Primary Unit of the Common Good
* Love and Care of Children
* Social, Communal Living Rather than Isolation
* Yearn for Truth and Shun Ignorance
* A Belief in God[48]

Some have argued that St. Thomas describes these levels of understanding by the terms "primary" and "secondary." In the first instance, the human agent knows without much application or thought, such as procreation and social living, self preservation and belief in God. This type of knowledge is often referred to as "self-evident." These are the primary—though there is some disagreement on the description.[49] Exactly where the primary evolves into the secondary is not always discernable. It seems a safe bet to argue that abortion, human inequality, homosexuality, suicide and murder will find a prominent place in the upper tier of natural law precepts. The difficulties emerge when we move, or better said, descend into particular problems. The secondary precepts of the natural law are sometimes labeled deductive, close, logical extensions of the primary or "derived from primary precepts."[50] The clarity of secondary and even tertiary natural law applications, St. Thomas says, suffers,

> Accordingly then in speculative matters truth is the same for all men, both as to principles and as to conclusions; although the truth is not known to all as regards the conclusions, but only as regards the principles which are called common notions. But in matters of action, truth or practical rectitude is not the same for all, as to matters of detail, but not as to the general principles: and where there is the same rectitude in matters of detail, it is not equally known by all.[51]

Even with particularity, a predictable struggle of interpretation often arises. The fact that primary precepts are self-evident makes them fundamentally non-negotiable. While there are only five or so of these propositions, it seems incongruous that natural law theory is labeled intrusive. St. Thomas shows no hesitation in giving permanency to the primary principles of the natural law—that speculative content, that knowledge of the obvious so to speak. Its objectivity rests on three fronts—first, its sameness for all human players. St. Thomas cannot envision any human agent not disposed to these fundamental activities, things like procreation, love, and the like. The list, as we have noted, is not very long, but it is universally shared. He states:

Consequently we must say that the natural law, as to general principles, is the same for all, both as to rectitude and as to knowledge.[52]

In addition to sameness, St. Thomas addresses changeability in the natural law—and for the most part he indicates that it does not really change at all, though we might be open to new interpretations consistent with the general principles. Thomas knows the particulars are always tougher than the general propositions and he allows for some variation as we move downwards in the level of difficulty. He notes:

In this sense, the natural law is altogether unchangeable in its first principles: but in the secondary principles … certain detailed proximate conclusions drawn from the first principles, the natural law is not changed so that what it prescribes be not right in most cases. But it may be changed in some particular cases of rare occurrence, through some special causes hindering the observance of such precepts …[53]

Finally, St. Thomas edifies the permanency of these first principles by indicating that the content of the natural law can never be eliminated, abolished or blotted out from the heart of man. It is an interesting choice of words for a philosopher so dedicated to reason and the intellect, although its choice indicates how integrated and intensely part of our being these tenets of the natural law really are. Just as some content of the natural law can be fully understood, in the lower level evaluations, St. Thomas argues that repetitive sin, or "corrupt and vicious habits"[54] can blot out our understanding.

Given these objective measures, Aquinas will conclude that any law, promulgated by man, that is inconsistent with these fundamental principles, will not be worthy of the name law, since it cannot bind or oblige us.[55] Promulgation for Aquinas is a process whereby "practical reason 'proceeds' from general principles of the natural law to the particular enactments of the positive law.[56] When antagonistic to the natural law St. Thomas indicates:

Consequently every human law has just so much the nature of a law, as it is derived from the law of nature. But if in any point it deflects from the law of nature, it is no longer a law but a perversion of law.[57]

As a result of this view, Aquinas will conclude that promulgations in opposition to the basic tenets of the natural law are not worthy of obedience, cannot bind or compel adherence and should be viewed as non-existent.

A jurisprudence of non-recognition constitutes a radical legal philosophy. Each case or legal dilemma need be evaluated in light of this radical approach. By way of illustration, laws which legalize abortion would falter on many fronts for St. Thomas. First, such a law would be inconsistent with reason itself, correct thinking in relation to our fundamental natures. Second, such a law would directly confront the self-preservation principle of the natural law. Finally, he would hold that, on balance, abortion practice has not been positive for the collective and the common good. As a result of these three flaws, St. Thomas would reject these laws as unjust, and second, non-existent promulgations that cannot bind or oblige. These conclusions would not be possible without an objective series of moral precepts discoverable in the natural law.

In the final analysis, a nation lacking an objective moral order is destined to fail; a decline caused by its own misunderstanding of truth and good, and an unwillingness to adjudge good and evil.

CHAPTER 5

The Compatibility of Aquinas and King

Introduction

It is almost self-evident that St. Thomas and Martin Luther King, Jr., are kindred spirits and upon close inspection their philosophy of civil disobedience rests upon identical moorings. Despite the chronological difference of nearly seven centuries, readers are impressed by the similarity of approach, the passion of the arguments, and inclination to see things metaphysically rather than temporally. Of course there are differences in style. St. Thomas argues as a physicist, hypothesizing and testing questions with both counter and complimentary arguments. Aquinas personifies the dialectic and is unafraid to pose arguments clearly out of the mainstream and often heretical for his time. St. Thomas relies heavily on the mind and method of Aristotle and it's fair to argue that he Christianizes Aristotle. He does even more than that. St. Thomas systematizes the arguments regarding law and civil disobedience. He gives clarity to a complex theory—step by step, argument by argument. While he relies on past figures, like Aristotle and Augustine, he develops a comprehensive body of text which foretells the arguments King will make during the Civil Rights era. It is prophetic beyond words with King posing his advocacy of civil disobedience as if he were the ghost of St. Thomas. However, King approaches the subject with a more humanistic and psychological feel.

While Thomas indicates that law need tend to the "good," or that law must habituate the citizenry towards virtue, King will speak of the "human personality" or how a law must "uplift," and develop a person holistically. It is a very complimentary tact though its pedagogy starkly different. In Thomas we witness the

91

"human person" as "being" or essence, each and everyone tending to their proper ends, yearning and searching for God and living in accordance with fundamental natures. Thomas speaks of the citizen as if a philosophical entity while King personalizes them. Much has been written about this "personalism" in King—this being his tendency to communicate about people very personally especially in light of the God who oversees us.[1] Indeed King's discussion of God is so intimate when compared to Aquinas, with God serving as guide and moral base for his Civil Rights movement. So, King will speak in highly personal tones about the Creator, an example being,

> God's unbroken hold on us is something that will never permit us to feel right when we do wrong or to feel natural when we do the unnatural.[2]

When King speaks of the Creator, he does so as proximate to God, accepting his Fatherly love and guidance in the temporal sphere, and treasured without "a graded scale of essential worth."[3]

Aquinas will reach the same conclusion, that God, the eternal law, is the starting point and any law inconsistent with the eternal promulgation is a law that need be disobeyed. St. Thomas, to compare the method, describes God as a "prime or first mover," a descriptor that hardly conjures up the intimacy that King displays. God for St. Thomas is only knowable by the effects of things in the universe, or a "motion" other than our type of motion—"something from potentiality to actuality."[4] God is, for Aquinas, devoid of motion and that being which as the "first mover, put in motion by no other; and this everyone understands to be God."[5]

King and Aquinas each find God to be the terminus and justification for all human action. Each, by using God as the centerpiece of their jurisprudence, provides an objective moral order for use in the assessment of ethical problems. Today, with ethical complexity everywhere, from cloning to post partum abortion, from same sex marriage to selective reduction, the world daily confronts the "binding" and "obligatoriness" of law in particular cases. The contemporary slavishness to positivism makes ethical inquiry quite foreign in legal analysis. A fresh look at St. Thomas Aquinas and

Martin Luther King, Jr., may bridge the chasm between law and a jurisprudence of the right and true.

Aquinas and King on the Nature of Law

In the question of what law is or means both King and Aquinas come to a similar conclusion. While St. Thomas will expend more energy on the role of reason, the common good and the content and substance of the natural law, each will deduce that a law can only be a law if it is consistent with a higher law. In King a law finds no legitimacy in the enactment alone and it is plain that King critiques the blind adherence to positivism. He will use other less refined terms when speaking of the "law" yet for the most part mimic Aquinas. Law must be consistent with our nature: it must "square" with the moral law of the universe, and not be contrary to the law of God. King's most famous passages from the *Letter from Birmingham Jail* summarizes his concept of law,

> A just law is a man made code that squares with the moral law or the law of God. An unjust law is a code out of harmony with the moral law. To put it in the terms of St. Thomas Aquinas: an unjust law is a human law that is not rooted in the eternal and natural law.[6]

For Aquinas, law is the "rule and measure" of reason. In other words, the intellect discovers law through correct thinking or as Cicero labeled it, "recta ratio"—right reason. Very few scholars on St. Thomas fully appreciate this insight with the primary emphasis always being on the content of the natural law. St. Thomas tells us, quite remarkably, if you think correctly you will be lawful. If you think correctly you will properly balance your emotions and passions, and tend to virtue over vice. This is an innovative form of psychology that King will pick up on. For King speaks of a person who becomes "degraded"[7] by unjust laws, suffering immensely not only due to the injustice itself but what the injustice does to the mind, or even more tellingly how the party inflicting the injustice fails to think too. In all of these senses, we see the intellec-

tual nature of law, that reason discovers and applies law pruden-
tially. King frequently applies this approach when he assesses the
heart and mind of the segregationist for the man or woman who
hates based on race, creed or color, is not a thinking man in the
least and surely not lawful in approach. This hate cannot be rooted
in reason but driven by errant emotion and vice. The segregationist cannot understand that King's adherents accept injustice
without vengeance, that they "turn to the left and the right and
catch a glimpse of divinity in the eyes of the other."[8]

In this fashion King and Aquinas agree regarding the definition
of law—that is the province of the intellect and not emotion.

Aquinas and King on Civil Disobedience

As to the legitimacy and ethicality of civil disobedience, King
and Aquinas fully concur. Unjust law cannot, St. Thomas says,
"bind" in conscience.

> Laws framed by man are either just or unjust. If they be
> just, they have the power of binding in conscience, from
> the eternal law whence they are derived. On the other
> hand, laws may be unjust.... Wherefore such laws do not
> bind in conscience.[9]

The fact that unjust laws do not bind produces two ramifications; first, that the law need not be obeyed if imposed or applicable to the moral actor, and second, that the citizen need not give
any credibility to the law and in fact must not "recognize" it as a
law at all.

St. Thomas urges his readers to initially determine whether a
law is just or not before engaging in civil disobedience. The virtue
"justice" serves as centerpiece in his theory of civil disobedience
because to be just is to give what is "due" another. Justice is relational, meaning that it depends upon human interaction. The justness or unjustness of any act is measured in a communal context.
As is his method, St. Thomas stresses justice as a virtue with special emphasis on how we measure human conduct. In particular,

St. Thomas describes justice as the "mean" for moral action—that is just acts neither harm anyone nor cause any harm to the common good. Just as compellingly, the mean applies to individuals living out lives in the collective. Just persons, St. Thomas says, live with their neighbors in justice.

> When a man does what he ought, he brings no gain to the person to whom he does what he ought, but only abstains from doing him harm. He does however profit himself, in so far as he does what he ought, spontaneously and readily, and this is to act virtuously.[10]

St. Thomas also uses Injustice as a tool of comparison. Unjust laws are, for St. Thomas, "not laws at all" and they do "violence" to our understanding of law. Under Thomas's view, an unjust law need not be "obeyed."

> Human law has the nature of law in so far as it partakes of right reason; and it is clear that, in this respect, it is derived from the eternal law. But in so far as it deviates from reason, it is called an unjust law, and has the nature, not of law but of violence.[11]

Herein lies the Thomistic theory of civil disobedience—that unjust laws are not worthy of our allegiance.

For King, the conclusion is the same, but the emphasis is quite a contrast. King expends little energy defining justice as a precept or a virtue. He affirms that unjust laws are inconsistent with the law of God.

> A just law is a manmade code that squares with the moral law or the law of God. An unjust law is a code that is out of harmony with the moral law. To put it in the terms of St. Thomas Aquinas: An unjust law is a human law that is not rooted in the eternal or natural law."[12]

His inclination is to weigh and assess injustice in the marketplace. How do unjust acts impact the citizenry? What effect does a particular law have upon the personal self worth of an individual? From this vantage point, King uses justice and injustice as a basis for whether civil disobedience is appropriate or not. Its use is not always easy to apply. King relates:

> I submit that an individual that breaks a law that conscience tells him is unjust, and who willingly accepts the penalty of imprisonment in order to arouse the conscience of the community over its injustice, is in reality expressing the highest respect for the law.[13]

Injustice must be countered with justice; injustice must be removed from the heart and mind of man and replaced with a love based on human dignity.[14] Civil disobedience is the means to correcting injustice and unjust laws and it is consistent with an overall ethic that insists that harm come to no one and injury be avoided at all costs. Civil disobedience, King argues, mirrors the greatestness of Christianity and the philosophy of Jesus Christ. Jesus is "a model for action and an inspiration to action."[15] As Christ has suffered on the Cross, so does the party engaged in civil disobedience whose suffering portrays a passionate righteousness about the cause at hand and should be considered "the model for human life and an inspiration for life."[16]

It is King's desire to change hearts and minds, to show the errors of the segregationist but to do so with moral authority. Civil disobedience is the only way to go. When St. Thomas spoke of the overthrow of tyrants, he reminded us that violence be a last resort and not the first choice for initiating change. Each thinker holds firm to a vision of nonviolence and the hope for change to emerge without raising a hand.

Aquinas and King on Civil Disobedience and the Christian Faith

The integration of a Christian philosophy into a theory of Civil Disobedience provides moral credibility to the advocate. As noted earlier, contemporary situation ethics suffers from a fluidity that delivers an ever changing basis for moral reasoning. Instead of an objective moral order, one derived from the omniscient and immutable God, modernists struggle with the inevitable variability of relative ethics. Nothing in relativity can ever be tied down and as a result, today's moral imperative can be whisked away by tomorrow's novelty. King and Aquinas fully recognize the need for a perennial philosophy to support their theory of civil disobedience.

For Aquinas, the entire legal superstructure, all laws, courts, lawyers and judges, legislators and bill makers need to remember the hierarchical content of the law; how that law is defined, where it is derived from, and, whether the enactment is consistent or inconsistent with a higher law. St. Thomas ties the very lowest low, enacted by the common man, with the very highest, the Eternal Law, that of the Godhead. He remarks,

> Since then the eternal law is the plan of government in the Chief Governor, all the plans in the inferior governors must be derived from the eternal law. But these plans of inferior governors are all other laws besides the eternal law. Therefore all laws, in so far as they partake of right reason, are derived from the eternal law.[17]

With God at the head of legal system, the citizen needs to display faith and recognize the central role a spiritual life plays in the activity of a moral agent. There is no separation of religion from the public square. God cannot be vanquished from the legislative hall or paneled courthouse. For Aquinas, a citizen must disobey the unjust law, must resist enactments contrary to the eternal and natural law, and must actively work to repeal unjust measures. St. Thomas convincingly relays,

> Accordingly all that is in things created by God, whether it be contingent or necessary, is subject to the eternal law.[18]

St. Thomas also stresses the role of the New Law—the law posed in the perfect charity of Jesus Christ. In Christ, St. Thomas discovers the purest good, love of neighbor and God the Father. Christ represents and encompasses the nature of redemption and salvation. Christ urges his followers to love without reservation, to forgive enemies, and to endure suffering. While rendering Caesar his due, Jesus insists that the citizen resist injustice and work to eliminate it. St. Thomas pulls in all that Christ has to offer in his theory of civil disobedience,

> So the complete fulfillment of the law depends on love, according to the text of the Apostle: "Love is the fulfilling of the law" (Rom. 3:10). And the Lord says that "on these two commandments," that is, love of God and of neighbor, "dependeth the whole law" (Matt. 22:40).[19]

As St. Thomas makes plain the role of a Christian philosophy in a theory of civil disobedience, so too will Dr. King stress the necessity of a Christian ethos in his justification for civil disobedience. For King, it is an affirmative obligation to resist unjust laws since these laws are in opposition to Christian tradition. King eloquently makes his case,

> The highest court of justice is in the heart of man when he is inspired by the teaching of Christ. Rather than being the judge, Christ is the light in which we pass judgment on ourselves. The truth is that every day our deeds and words, our silence and speech are building character. Any day that reveals this fact is a day of judgment.[20]

In the language of King, government should seek to become a "beloved community," a Kingdom on earth, rooted in justice. A Kingdom that God chose—a "site on which to build a wonderful structure, a global union of real brothers sharing in his good gifts, and offering all achievement as a form of worship to him."[21] In Christ, the true meaning of human existence is discoverable. In Christ, notions of human equality and human justice become clear and straightforward. In Christ, King discerns the perfect sacrifice and the doorway to salvation. In Christ, King finds the role model for suffering and atonement for "speaking the truth, seeking the truth and defending the truth."[22] King reminds his followers that the road to Christian civil disobedience is pathed with many challenges.

> I am impelled to write you concerning the responsibilities laid upon you to live as Christians in the midst of an un-

Christian world. That is what I had to do. That is what every Christian has to do. But I understand that there are many Christians in America that give their ultimate allegiance to man-made systems and customs. They are afraid to be different.[23]

In this sense, King calls upon the Christian to stand up and resist, not because they do not like this or that about a particular law, but because they must resist and seek to overturn the promulgation. The Christian is obliged to topple the injustice. King sums it up keenly.

It is not the violence of the sword or stone that will recaste and reshape the world, but the liberation that only comes from Christian love and the Gospel values of Jesus Christ.[24]

Aquinas and King on Non-Recognition

The principle of Non-Recognition is quite radical since it exhorts complete objection to a promulgated law. This principle is radical because, aside from the objection to the law itself, there is a call for complete rejection of the law being a law at all. Most people fail to appreciate the nuance. Advocates of civil disobedience usually conclude that some laws are simply unjust. The Thomist takes it a step further by holding that this type of law does not exist, it cannot be labeled law and as such, compliance is not required. King was, for the most part, in the former school, often railing against specific laws as being unjust. In a few places he argues the Augustinian maxim, "that an unjust law is not a law at all" and simultaneously cites St. Thomas. Comparatively, St. Thomas emphasizes that a law inconsistent with the eternal and the natural law fails to bind in conscience and is in fact not a law in any sense. Law, as a rule and measure of reason, can only be law when consistent with the content of the natural law which is deposited and part of reason, and this natural law is the imprint of the Creator. St. Thomas holds that law,

[H]as a share of the Eternal Reason, whereby it has a natural inclination to its proper act and end; and this participation of the eternal law in the rational creature is called the natural law...It is therefore evident that the natural law is nothing else than the rational creature's participation in the eternal law.[25]

Here lies the radical nature of his jurisprudence—that I need not recognize it, nor comply with its mandate or provisions, and as a result of these conclusions, affirmatively must not abide by its provisions. In Aquinas we see not only an intellectual act, but the motion of resistance. To not comply is to resist.

As the Apostle says (Rom. Xiii, 1, 2) all human power is from God.... 'therefore he that resisteth the power,' in matters that are within its scope, 'resisteth the ordinance of God,'; so that he becomes guilty according to his conscience.[26]

King's stress is the resistaqnce itself, rather than dwelling on non-recognition. In a more particular way, King lays out specific steps, specific actions that should be taken by the resistor. Sit in's, walk in's, boarding buses, eating at segregated counters, drinking from prohibited water fountains are just some examples of this action, this motion of resistance. King uses civil disobedience as the catalyst for change. He notes,

The purpose of our direct-action program is to create a situation so crisis packed that it will inevitably open the door to negotiation.[27]

Agitation with love accurately describes King's methodology. In King's circle, agitation will trigger suffering and the sacrifice of those engaging in civil disobedience. King recognizes the "necessity of suffering"[28] in the movement. Despite this activism, one gets the sense that King still believes these laws exist however unjust they might be. King always speaks of laws as if promulgated even though utterly wrong in design. St. Thomas seems to go a step further by applying the principle of non-recognition with full force. St. Thomas believes that these laws have no reality, and on the other hand King sees these laws in the most brutal context. He experiences injustice first hand. So it could be argued that St. Thomas argues in a more theoretical way while King argues in the muck of the streets. Either way, they reach the fundamental conclusion that no allegiance is owed to an unjust law. One need not follow or abide by its provisions. St. Thomas issues a radical theory of non-existence relative to the unjust law. The implications are extraordinary and yet to be fully tested.

The Relevance of Aquinas and King

The complexities of modern ethical questions highlight our present incapacity to affect ethical resolutions. We live in a culture run wild with ethical dilemmas—from same sex marriage to abortion, from cloning to physician assisted suicide. Interestingly, many of today's pressing moral problems were outside the timeline of Martin Luther King. Even more curiously, Aquinas dealt with abortion, homosexuality, sodomy and the parameters of marriage 700 years earlier. By 1960, these moral quandaries had yet to coalesce and this was in large part to a more unified, collective outlook on these practices. King's record on these questions is scant, though his surviving daughter, Andrea, has become a national critic of abortion.[29] During King's lifetime, given the consensus on homosexuality, abortion, and the futuristic qualities of cloning and the like, the disobedience was naturally targeted to questions involving equality.

For contemporary moralists, most of the dialogue and debate concerning these troublesome questions usually invites a "right" stripped of traditional ethical reasoning. Surely arguments about rights have become almost dreary. In a word, there is a right to everything. Individualism has replaced all sensibility regarding the common good. There are no universals; no certitude in moral propositions; no moral code fixed and perennial. All of this has been replaced with the immediacy of any need and the whining of the moment. Today's rights are replaced with tomorrow's method of control. Rights last as long as the next plea from a crying advocate. Of course, this approach is what gave us slavery. Instead of evaluating the practice of slavery in universal moral terms, based upon a perennial notion of truth, history generates all the excuses of why we need slavery. In the pre-Civil War period, the arguments were about money and economics, sub-humans and property, not the stuff of Thomistic reason.

In the final analysis, there is nothing in modern positivism that can resolve ethical issues. Positivism is simply too fleeting. Positivism has no anchor only ticking time which awaits the next alarm. Therefore, in the modern world view, if our legislature tells us that cloning is good, so be it. If it changes its mind, so shall it be. And on and on the ethical wheel goes.

Both King and Aquinas deliver an ethical construct that mirrors human life. Both King and Aquinas posit ethical principles rooted in perennial principles that can be relied upon in all cases. For St. Thomas, it will be about the law of nature and the natural law. In the first instance, we decipher what is good for us as beings. In the second instance, we apply the Creator's principles, fully imprinted in our psyche—to tend to the good, to procreate, to marry, to live in community, to believe in a God and to preserve our lives.

For King, it will be about our advancement, our growth, our development as human beings. King applies a humanist, personalist touch to all these issues but the terminus is identical to St. Thomas. King will also evaluate the compatibility of any human law with his "higher law" jurisprudence. He will look for and crave consistency in the human enactment with the law of God. He will demand consistency in what we do as humans with what God expects from us. He will evaluate whether a proposed law "uplifts" the human person or undermines its essence.

All of this goes a long way to providing a blueprint to human action and assuring life, liberty, and the dignity of the human person.

Notes

Preface

1. 2 Thomas Aquinas, Summa Theologica, English Dominican Friars, trans., II-II, Q. 96, a 4, 1019 (1948). Susan Teifenbrun, *Civil Disobedience and the U.S Constitution*, 32 Sw. L. Rev. 680 (2003).
2. Martin Luther King, Jr., The Triumph of Conscience 74 (1967).
3. James T. McHugh, *The Value of a Religiously Affiliated Law School*, 74 St. John's L. Rev. 579 (2000).
4. 2 Martin Luther King, Jr., The Papers of Martin Luther King: Rediscovering Precious Values 120 (1994).
5. Martin Luther King, Jr., Letter from Birmingham Jail 6 (April 16, 1963), http://www.stanford.edu/group/King/speeches.
6. Aquinas, *supra* note 1 at II-II, Q. 96, a 4, 1020.
7. Martin Luther King. Jr., Strength to Love 105 (1963).
8. King, *supra* note 5 at 6.
9. 1 Thomas Aquinas, Summa Theologica, English Dominican Friars, trans., I-II, Q. 93, a 3, 1005 (1948).

Chapter 1

1. Martin Luther King, Jr., Strength to Love 23 (1963).
2. Martin Luther King, Jr., The Triumph of Conscience 48 (1967).
3. *Id.* at 8.
4. For an interesting examination of how constitutional interpretation takes place with or without natural law reasoning *see* Lee J. Strang, *The Clash of Rival and Incompatible Philosophical Tradi-*

tions within Constitutional Interpretation: Originalism and the Aristotelian Tradition, 2 GEO. J. LAW & PUB. POL'Y 523 (2004).

5. Robert Goodwin, *Aquinas Justice: An Interpretation*, 63 NEW SCHOLASTICISM 275 (1989).

6. KARL KREILKAMP, THE METAPHYSICAL FOUNDATIONS OF THOMISTIC JURISPRUDENCE 115 (1939).

7. J.V. Dolan, *Natural Law and Modern Jurisprudence*, 16 LAVAL THEOLOGIQUE ET PHILOSOPHIQUE 40 (1960).

8. 2 THOMAS AQUINAS, "SUMMA THEOLOGICA," BASIC WRITINGS OF SAINT THOMAS AQUINAS, Anton C. Pegis, ed., II-II, Q. 96 (1945).

9. *Id.* at II-II, Q. 96. *See Also* Mark R. Macguigan, *Civil Disobedience And Natural Law*, 52 KY. L. J. 347-362 (1964); Howard Zinn, *Law, Justice and Disobedience*, NOTRE DAME J. L. ETHICS & PUB. POL'Y 899-919 (1991).

10. *See* John Finnis, *Unjust Laws In A Democratic Society: Some Philosophical And Theological Reflections*, 71 NOTRE DAME L. REV. 595 (1995-1996); Anthony E. Cook, *Beyond Critical Legal Studies: The Reconstruction Theology Of Dr. Martin Luther King, Jr.*, 103 HARVARD L. REV. 985 (1990); David Benjamin Oppenheimer, *Martin Luther King, Walker v. City Of Birmingham, And The Letter From The Birmingham Jail*, 26 U.C. DAVIS L. REV. 791 (1993).

11. Aquinas, *supra* note 2 at *I-II*, Q. 96, a. 4.

12. Aquinas, *supra* note 2 at *I-II*, Q. 96, a. 4, c.

13. Aquinas, *supra* note 2 at *I-II*, Q. 96, a. 4, c.

14. Aquinas, *supra* note 2 at *I-II*, Q. 96, a. 4, ad. 2.

15. Aquinas, *supra* note 2 at *I-II*, Q. 96, a. 4, ad. 2.

16. Aquinas, *supra* note 2 at *I-II*, Q. 95, a. 2, Q. 96, a. 4.

17. Aquinas, *supra* note 2 at *I-II*, Q. 96, a. 4, c.

18. Aquinas, *supra* note 2 at *I-II*, Q. 96, a. 2, ad. 2.

19. Igor Grazin, *Natural Law As A Form Of Legal Studies*, 37 AM. J. JURIS. 37 (1992).

20. Noel Dermot O'Donoghue, *The Law Beyond The Law*, 18 AM. J. JURIS. 164 (1973).

21. J.V. Dolan, *Natural Law and Judicial Function*, 16 LAVAL THEOLOGIQUE ET PHILOSOPHIQUE 96-97 (1960).

22. THOMAS AQUINAS, COMMENTARY ON THE NICOMACHEAN ETHICS 931 (1964).

23. Daniel Nelson, The Priority of Prudence 107 (1992). *See also* Daniel J. Sullivan, An Introduction to Philosophy, The Perennial Principles of Classical Realist Tradition (1992); Bernard Beodder, S.J., Natural Theology (1927); Etienne Gilson, The Christian Philosophy of St. Thomas Aquinas, trans. L.K. Shook, 266 (1956); Thomas E. Davitt, The Nature of Law 39-54 (1951).

24. 4 Thomas Aquinas, Summa Contra Gentiles, trans. Vernon J. Bourke, Book III, part II, Chapter 114, 1 (1975).

25. Anton-Hermann Chroust, *The Philosophy of Law of St. Thomas Aquinas: His Fundamental Ideas and Some of His Historical Precursors*, 19 Am. J. Juris. 24 (1974).

26. Gilson, *supra* note 23 at 266.

27. Aquinas, *supra* note 24 at III-II, 115.

28. *Id.* at III-II, 114.

29. *Id.* at III-II, 114.

30. Aquinas, *supra* note 2 at I-II, Q. 90, a. 1, sed contra.

31. Aquinas, *supra* note 2 at I-II, Q. 90, a. 1, ad 1.

32. Aristotle, Physics, *II*, 9 (200a 22); Aquinas, *supra* note 2 at I-II, Q. 90, a. 1, c.

33. Aquinas, *supra* note 2 at I-II, Q. 96, a. 2, c.

34. Aquinas, *supra* note 2 at I-II, Q. 96, a. 1, ad 2.

35. Aquinas, *supra* note 2 at I-II, Q. 96, a. 2.

36. Aquinas, *supra* note 2 at I-II, Q. 90, art. 2, c.

37. Jeremy Bentham, The Principles of Morals and Legislation (1948).

38. Dolan, *supra* note 7 at 16.

39. *Id.* at 40.

40. Anton-Hermann Chroust, *The Fundamental Ideas in St Augustine's Philosophy of Law*, 18 Am. J. Juris. 67 (1973).

41. Daniel Nelson appreciates this comprehensive view of law when he states, "Law in all of its manifestations derives from God's reason." Nelson, *supra* note 23 at 107. *See also Id.* at 67.

42. Aquinas, *supra* note 24 at III-II, Ch. 112, 3.

43. Thomas Aquinas, The Treatise on Law, ed. R. J. Henle 149 (1993).

44. Aquinas, *supra* note 2 at I-II, Q. 93, a. 3, sed contra.

45. *Id.*

46. Gilson, *supra* note 23 at 266.

47. Chroust, *supra* note 25 at 25.

48. Aquinas, *supra* note 2 at I-II, Q. 93, a. 1.

49. Aquinas, *supra* note 2 at I, Q. 45, a. 3.

50. Aquinas, *supra* note 2 at I-II, Q. 93, a. 1, c.

51. Aquinas, *supra* note 2 at I-II, Q. 93, a. 1, c.

52. Aquinas, *supra* note 2 at I-II, Q. 91, a. 1.

53. Aquinas, *supra* note 2 at I-II, Q. 93, a. 2, ad. 1.

54. Aquinas, *supra* note 2 at I-II, Q. 93, a. 4, c.

55. Aquinas, *supra* note 2 at I-II, Q. 91, a. 1, c.

56. Aquinas, *supra* note 2 at I-II, Q. 91, a. 1, c.

57. Aquinas, *supra* note 2 at I-II, Q. 93, a. 6, ad. 3.

58. Aquinas, *supra* note 2 at I-II, Q. 93, a. 6, ad. 2.

59. Aquinas, *supra* note 2 at I-II, Q. 93, a. 6, ad. 2.

60. Aquinas, *supra* note 2 at I-II, Q. 93, a. 1, ad. 3.

61. C.S. LEWIS, STUDIES IN WORDS 37 (1960).

62. *Id.* at 24.

63. ST. THOMAS AQUINAS, ON KINGSHIP, ch. II, 19.

64. BERNARD BORDER, S.J., NATURAL THEOLOGY 46 (1927).

65. Gilson, *supra* note 23 at 266.

66. Alasdair MacIntyre's often cited work, *Whose Justice? Which Rationality?*, warns the critic and ally alike that the natural law is not merely a registry of pre- and proscriptions. "Obeying the precepts of the natural law is more than simply refraining from doing what those precepts prohibit and doing what they enjoin. The precepts become effectively operative only as and when we find ourselves with motivating reasons for performing actions inconsistent with those precepts; what the precepts can then provide us with is a reason which can outweigh the motivating reasons for disobeying them, that is, they point us to a more perfect good than do the latter." ALASDAIR MACINTYRE, WHOSE JUSTICE? WHICH RATIONALITY? 194 (1988).

67. Aquinas, *supra* note 2 at I-II, Q. 94, a. 1.

68. Aquinas, *supra* note 2 at I-II, Q. 91, a. 2, c.

69. Aquinas, *supra* note 2 at I-II, Q. 91, a. 2, c.

70. IGNATIUS T. ESCHMANN, THE ETHICS OF ST. THOMAS AQUINAS 187 (1997).

71. *Id.* at 166-67.
72. Aquinas, *supra* note 2 at I-II, Q. 94, a. 6.
73. Aquinas, *supra* note 2 at I-II, Q. 94, a. 2, c.
74. Aquinas, *supra* note 24 at III-I, ch. 4, 2.
75. Aquinas, *supra* note 24 at III-I, ch. 6, 5.
76. Aquinas, *supra* note 2 at I-II, Q. 94, a. 2, ad. 2.
77. *See* BRIAN TIERNEY, THE IDEA OF NATURAL RIGHTS: STUD-IES ON NATURAL RIGHTS, NATURAL LAW AND CHURCH LAW 1150-1625 (1998).
78. Aquinas, *supra* note 2 at I-II, Q. 94, a. 4, c.
79. Aquinas, *supra* note 2 at I-II, Q. 94, a. 4, ad. 3.
80. Aquinas, *supra* note 2 at I-II, Q. 98, a. 1, c.
81. Jean Tonneau, *The Teaching of the Thomist Tract on Law*, 31 THE THOMIST 34 (1970).
82. Henle, *supra* note 43 at 172.
83. Aquinas, *supra* note 24 at III-II, ch. 116, 3.
84. Aquinas, *supra* note 2 at I-II, Q. 91, a. 4.
85. Aquinas, *supra* note 2 at I-II, Q. 91, a. 4, c.
86. Aquinas, *Theologica, Pegis, I-II*, Q. 99, a. 4, ad. 1.
87. For some well-grounded discussion of positive law in Thomistic jurisprudence *see* VINCENT McNABB, ST. THOMAS AQUINAS AND LAW (1955) and Barry F. Smith, *Of Truth and Certainty in the Law: Reflections on the Legal Method*, 30 AM. J. JURIS. 119 (1985).
88. Aquinas, *supra* note 2 at I-II, Q., 95, a. 1.
89. Aquinas, *supra* note 2 at I-II, Q., 95, a. 1.
90. Charles Skok portrays Thomas' vision as realistic rather than pessimistic. "St. Thomas often made reference to men in their present condition. Not many men are truly virtuous or highly virtuous. Laws have to be made for the general run of the people in the state in which they are found. This is not pessimism but realism." CHARLES D. SKOK, PRUDENT CIVIL LEGISLATION ACCORDING TO ST. THOMAS AND SOME CONTROVERSIAL AMERICAN LAW 119 (1967).
91. Aquinas, *supra* note 2 at I-II, Q. 95, a. 1, ad. 1.
92. Aquinas, *supra* note 2 at I-II, Q. 95, a. 3.
93. Aquinas, *supra* note 2 at I-II, Q. 95, a. 4, c.

94. Henle, *supra* note 43 at 335.

95. Aquinas, *supra* note 2 at I-II, Q. 96, a. 5, c.

96. Aquinas, *supra* note 2 at I-II, Q. 105, a. 1, ad. 5.

97. Aquinas, *supra* note 2 at I-II, Q. 99, a. 6, ad. 2.

98. Aquinas, *supra* note 2 at I-II, Q. 91, a. 2, ad. 2.

99. Aquinas, *supra* note 2 at I-II, Q. 95, a. 2, c.

100. M. Gilson, Law on The Human Level: Moral Values and Moral life The System of St. Thomas, L. Ward trans., 204 (1931).

101. Aquinas, *supra* note 2 at I-II, Q. 93, a. 3. 2.

102. Aquinas, *supra* note 2 at I-II, Q. 93, a. 3.

103. Aquinas, *supra* note 2 at I-II, Q. 93, a. 3, ad. 1.

104. Aquinas, *supra* note 2 at I-II, Q. 93, a. 3, ad. 2.

105. Aquinas, *supra* note 2 at I-II, Q. 96, a. 2, ad. 2.

106. Aquinas, *supra* note 2 at I-II, Q. 96, a. 2, ad. 3.

107. Raymond Dennehy addresses the law's ultimate aim in *The Ontological Basis of Human Rights.* "For, as a rational being, man attains his self-perfection by transcending the limitations of his finite, temporal self. Through the immanence of knowing, he achieves ever higher levels of reality as he identifies himself ontologically with Being and its facets. Truth, Goodness, Beauty, and ultimately with the fullness of Being, God; and all the while he retains his own unique selfhood." Raymond Dennehy, *The Ontological Basis of Human Rights*, 42 The Thomist 455, 456-57 (1978).

108. Rommen 54-55.

109. Aquinas, *supra* note 2 at I-II, Q. 96, a. 2. 213.

110. King, *supra* note 1 at 22.

111. *Id.* at 22.

112. 2 The Papers of Martin Luther King, Jr., Rediscovering Precious Values: July 1951-November 1955, 213 (1994).

113. For a full understanding of Aquinas, one must think and argue as Aristotle did. There is no secret of the reverence and awe that Aquinas holds for Aristotle. At no place is this more evident than in Aristotle's analysis of how virtue and the law intersect- a view fully adopted by St. Thomas. *See* Aristotle, Nicomachean Ethics 198, Hippocrates G. Apostle, trans., (1984).

114. *Id.* at 23.

115. King, *supra* note 112 at 217.

116. MARTIN LUTHER KING, JR., A KNOCK AT MIDNIGHT 67 (1998); Robert Sirico's highlights the inadequacy of a "rights" system based solely on human invention at *Civil Rights and Social Cooperation*, 11 REGENT UNIV. L.R. 10 (1998).

117. *Walker v. City of Birmingham*, 388 U.S 307 (1967).

118. Segregationist policies included a great deal of territory including but not limited to fountains, bathrooms, dressing rooms, schools, restaurants, hospitals, cemeteries to name just a few. *See* David Benjamin Oppenheimer, *Martin Luther King, Walker v. City of Birmingham, and the Letter from the Birmingham Jail,"* 26 U.C. DAVIS L. REV. 797 (1993).

119. King, *supra* note 116 at 96.

120. *Id.* at 96.

121. King, *supra* note 112 at 193.

122. Mark R. MacGuigan, *Civil Disobedience and the Natural Law*, 52 KY. L. J. 346 (1963-1964).

123. MARTIN LUTHER KING, JR., I'VE BEEN TO THE MOUNTAINTOP 11 (1994).

124. *Id.* at 11.

125. King, *supra* note 1 at 90.

126. *Id.* at 90.

127. *Id.* at 91.

128. King, *supra* note 112 at 57.

129. King, *supra* note 1 at 104.

130. MARTIN LUTHER KING, JR., WHERE DO WE GO FROM HERE: CHAOS OR COMMUNITY 84 (1968).

131. *Id.* at 84.

132. *Id.*

Chapter 2

1. Robert M. Palumbos, *Within Each Lawyer's Conscience a Touchstone: Law, Morality, and Attorney Civil Disobedience*, 153 U. PA. L. REV. 1058 (2005).

2. 1 THOMAS AQUINAS, SUMMA THEOLOGICA, English Dominican Friars, trans., I-II, Q.95, a.2, 1014 (1948); *See also* John Finnis, *Unjust Laws in a Democratic Society: Some Philosophical and Theological Reflections*, 71 NOTRE DAME L. REV. 595 (1995–1996).

3. Blake D. Morant, *Lesson from Thomas More's Dilemma of Conscience: Reconciling the Clash Between a Lawyer's Beliefs and Professional Expectations*, 78 ST. JOHN'S L. REV. 979 (2004).

4. CHARLES P. NEMETH, AQUINAS IN THE COURTROOM 74 (2001).

5. Aquinas, *supra* note 2 at Q. 96, a 4, 1019.

6. MARTIN LUTHER KING, JR., LETTER FROM BIRMINGHAM JAIL 4 (April 16, 1963), http://www.stanford.edu/group/King/speeches.

7. *Id.*

8. *Id.*

9. *Id.*

10. *Id.*

11. Susan Tiefenbrun, *Semiotics and Martin Luther King, Jr.'s Letter from the Birmingham Jail*, 4 CARDOZO STUD. L. & LITERATURE 273 (1992).

12. King, *supra* note 6 at 4.

13. MARTIN LUTHER KING, JR., *I Have a Dream, in* A CALL TO CONSCIENCE: THE LANDMARK SPEECHES OF DR. MARTIN LUTHER KING, JR., (August 28, 1963), http://www.stanford.edu/group/King/speeches.

14. MARTIN LUTHER KING, *Where Do We Go From Here: Chaos or Community?* (1967).

15. Alasdair McIntyre ably points out how justice is encased in the divine exemplar. "In its primary application 'Justice' is one of the names applied to God… It is not of course that it is by reference to this divine exemplar that *we* acquire the concept of justice; Aquinas' theory of concept-acquisition was Aristotelian, not Platonist, in its starting point, although it moved beyond Aristotle. But that there is such a timeless standard of justice is a claim ultimately grounded on a theological understanding of the ordering of things." ALASDAIR MACINTYRE, WHOSE JUSTICE? WHICH RATIONALITY? (1988).

16. James F. Ross, *Justice is Reasonableness: Aquinas on Human Law and Morality*, 58 THOMIST 100 (1974).
17. Aquinas, *supra* note 2 at I, Q 105, a 5, 519.
18. *Id.* at I, Q. 105, a. 2. c, 515.
19. Aquinas, *supra* note 2 at I-II, Q. 96, a. 2, 1018.
20. 2 THOMAS AQUINAS, SUMMA THEOLOGICA, English Dominican Friars, trans., II-II, Q. 58, a. 8, 1440 (1948).
21. *Id.* at II-II, Q. 58, a. 9, 1441.
22. *Id.* at, II-II, Q. 58, a. 11, c, 1442.
23. ALASDAIR MACINTYRE, WHOSE JUSTICE? WHICH RATIONALITY? (1988).
24. JAIME VELEZ SAENZ, THE DOCTRINE OF THE COMMON GOOD OF CIVIL SOCIETY IN THE WORKS OF ST. THOMAS AQUINAS 57 (1961).
25. THOMAS AQUINAS, COMMENTARY ON THE NICOMACHEAN ETHICS, C. I. Litzinger, trans., (1964). ARISTOTLE, NICOMACHEAN ETHICS, Martin Ostwald, trans., (1962).
26. Aquinas, *id.* at V. L.X: C 998.
27. Aquinas, *supra* note 20 at II-II, Q. 64, a. 1, 1466.
28. 2 THOMAS AQUINAS, "SUMMA THEOLOGICA," BASIC WRITINGS OF SAINT THOMAS AQUINAS, Anton C. Pegis, ed., I-II, Q. 64, a. 1, 468 (1945).
29. ETIENNE GILSON, THE CHRISTIAN PHILOSOPHY OF ST. THOMAS AQUINAS, L.K. Shook, trans., 264 (1956).
30. Aquinas, *supra* note 20 at II-II, Q. 58, a. 10, c, 1441.
31. *Id.* at II-II, Q. 58, a. 8, 1440.
32. J. MESSNER, SOCIAL ETHICS: NATURAL LAW IN THE MODERN WORLD, J.J. Doherty trans., 213 (1952).
33. Aquinas, *supra* note 20 at II-II, Q. 64, a. 2, c, 1467.
34. THOMAS AQUINAS, ON ARISTOTLE'S LOVE AND FRIENDSHIP, Pierre Conway, trans., IX, ch. 2 (1951).
35. Aquinas, *supra* note 2 at I-II, Q. 64, a. 1, 1466.
36. E. T. Gelinas, *Right and Law in Thomas Aquinas, in* 45 MYTH AND PHILOSOPHY, 132, 132 (George F. McLean ed., 1971).
37. Aquinas, *supra* note 20 at II-II, Q. 58, a. 9, 1441.
38. *Id.* at II-II, Q. 59, a. 1, 1443.
39. *Id.* at II-II, Q. 59, a. 1, 1443.

40. *Id.* at II-II, Q. 59, a. 4, 1449.

41. *Id.* at II-II, Q. 59, a. 3, 1448.

42. *Id.* at II-II, Q. 59, a. 2, 1444.

43. *Id.* at II-II, Q. 60, a. 6, 1450.

44. Messner, *supra* note 32 at 219.

45. Aquinas, *supra* note 25 at V. L.II: C 929.

46. *Id.* at V. L.II: C 930.

47. Aquinas, *supra* note 20 at II-II, Q. 61, a. 2, c, 1453.

48. *Id.* at II-II, Q. 61, a. 2. c, 1453.

49. *Id.* at II-II, Q. 61, a. 2. c, 1453.

50. *Id.* at II-II, Q. 61, a. 2. c, 1453.

51. *Id.* at II-II, Q. 66, a. 7, 1480.

52. Messner, *supra* note 32 at 218.

53. Aquinas, *supra* note 20 at II-II, Q. 61, a. 3, 1453.

54. *Id.* at II-II, Q. 61, a. 3, 1453.

55. *Id.* at II-II, Q. 66, a. 7. c, 1480.

56. "In cases of need all things are common property, so that there would seem to be no sin in taking another's property, for need has made it common." *Id.* at II-II, Q. 66, a. 7, 1480, sed contra.

57. Thomas Aquinas, The Treatise on Law, R. J. Henle ed., 72 (1993).

58. *See* Jean Porter, The Recovery of Virtue 53 (1990).

59. Morant, *supra* note 3 at 978.

60. Raymond Dennehy, *The Ontological Basis of Rights*, 42 Thomist 450 (1978).

61. Morant, *supra* note 3 at 979.

62. Walter Farrell, The Natural Moral Law: According to St. Thomas and Suarez 4 (1930).

63. Vernon Bourke, *Justice as Equitable Reciprocity*, 19 Am. J. Juris. 27 (1982).

64. Aquinas, *supra* note 2 at I-II, Q. 99, a. 5, 1035.

65. Paul Butler, *By Any Means Necessary: Using Violence and Subversion to Change Unjust Law*, 50 UCLA L. Rev. 752 (2003).

66. *Id.* at 748.

67. Martin Luther King, Jr., *Meet the Press, in* Boston University Collection I, 17 (NBC television broadcast April 17, 1960).

68. James P. Hanigan, Martin Luther Jr., and the Foundations of Nonviolence 237 (1984).

69. Keith D. Miller, Voice of Deliverance: The Language of Martin Luther King, Jr., and its Sources 92 (1992).

70. Lewis V. Baldwin, The Legacy of Martin Luther King, Jr.,: The Boundaries of Law, Politics and Religion 215 (2002).

71. Thomas Aquinas, On Kingship: To the King of Cyprus 25 (1982).

72. *Id.* at 26.

73. *Id.* at 26.

74. *Id.* at 24.

75. *Id.* at 25.

76. King, *supra* note 14 at 42.

77. Mark Edward DeForrest, *Civil Disobedience: Its Nature and Role in the American Legal Landscape,* 33 Gonzaga L. Rev. 657 (1997–1998).

78. James P. Hanigan, Martin Luther King, Jr., and the Foundations of Nonviolence 252–255 (1984).

79. Martin Luther King, Jr., Why We Can't Wait? 85 (1964).

80. Aquinas, *supra* note 20 at II-II, Q. 95, a. 3, 1015.

81. Hanigan, *supra* note 78 at 248.

82. *Id.* at 251.

83. *Id.* at 254.

84. Martin Luther King, Jr., The Power of Nonviolence, (June 4, 1957), http://www.teachingamericanhistory.org/library/index.asp?document=1131.

85. Hanigan, *supra* note 78.

86. Aquinas, *supra* note 20 at II-II, Q. 93, a. 3, 1004.

87. Hanigan, *supra* note 78 at 251.

88. King, *supra* note 84.

89. Martin Luther King, Jr., *A Christmas Sermon on Peace, in* A Testament of Hope, 122 (Washington, ed., 1991).

90. Baldwin, *supra* note 70 at 193.

91. 3 Thomas Aquinas, Summa Theologica, English Dominican Friars, trans., II-III, 1279 (1948).

92. *Id.* at II-III, 1295.

93. Aquinas, *supra* note 20 at II-II, 1295.

94. Aquinas, *supra* note 20 at II-II, 1293.

95. Martin Luther King, Jr.,*The Negro and the Constitution*, in THE CORNELLIAN (May 1944) http://www.stanford.edu/group/King/publications/papers/vol1/440500-The_Negro_and_the_Constitution.htm.

96. Hanigan, *supra* note 78 at 82.

97. *Id.* at 83.

98. Aquinas, *supra* note 91 at III, 2159.

99. DeForrest, *supra* note 77 at 658.

100. Aquinas, *supra* note 2 at I-II, Q. 95, a. 4, 1020.

101. *Id.* at I-II, Q. 95, a. 4 at 1020.

102. Butler, *supra* note 65 at 766b.

103. Aquinas, *supra* note 2 at I-II, Q. 95, a. 4 at 1020

104. Aquinas, *supra* note 71 at 24.

105. *Id.*

106. *Id.* at 27.

107. King, *supra* note 6.

108. MARTIN LUTHER KING, JR., *I've Been to the Mountaintop*, in A CALL TO CONSCIENCE: THE LANDMARK SPEECHES OF DR. MARTIN LUTHER KING, JR., (April 3, 1968) http://www.stanford.edu/group/King/speeches.

109. Baldwin, *supra* note 70 at 174.

110. *Id.*

111. Hanigan, *supra* note 78 at 248.

112. MARTIN LUTHER KING, JR., *Our Struggle, in* BOSTON UNIVERSITY COLLECTION V, 177.

113. Baldwin, *supra* note 70 at 243.

114. King, *supra* note 13 at 2.

115. King, *supra* note 6 at 5.

116. *Id.* at 6.

117. *Id.* at 4.

118. *Id.* at 8.

119. King, *supra* note 13 at 2.

120. DeForrest, *supra* note 77 at 659.

121. Aquinas, *supra* note 91 at III, Q. 49, a. 3, 2290.

122. Aquinas, *supra* note 91 at II-III, Q. 104, a. 6, 1646.

123. *Id.* at II-III, Q. 104, a. 5, 1645.

124. *Id.* at II-III, Q. 104, a. 6, 1646.

Chapter 3

1. Michael P Zuckert, *Do Natural Rights Come From Natural Law*, 20 Harvard J. L. & Pub. Pol'y 702 (1997).

2. R. J. Araujo, *Thomas Aquinas: Prudence, Justice and the Law*, 40 Loyola L. Rev. 897 (1995).

3. Martin Luther King, Jr., Letter from Birmingham Jail 8 (April 16, 1963), http://www.stanford.edu/group/King/speeches.

4. Charles D. Skok, Prudent Civil Legislation According to St. Thomas and Some Controversial American Law 117 (1967).

5. *Id.*

6. Dr. Martin Luther King, Jr., was acutely aware of a state or system of rights built on the atheist credo. In assessing Jacques Maritain, he seems to agree with "Communism arose as a revolt against Christianity itself." *See* 1 Martin Luther King, Jr., The Papers of Martin Luther King: Called to Serve 437 (1994).

7. 2 Martin Luther King, Jr., The Papers of Martin Luther King: Rediscovering Precious Values 217 (1994).

8. John T. Noonan, Jr, *The Tensions and the Ideals in Religious Human Rights in Global Perspective*, L. Perspectives 594–595 (1996).

9. Patrick McKinley Brennan, *Free Exercise! Following Conscience, Developing Doctrine and Opening Politics*, 74 Notre Dame L. Rev. 962 (1999).

10. Patrick M. J. Clancy, *St. Thomas on Law, in* 3 Summa Theologica 3270 (English Dominican Friars, trans., 1947).

11. *See* Coretta Scott King, My Life with Martin Luther King, Jr. (1969). His spouse reflects on these tensions and indicates that Gandhi held enormous sway over King upon a return from a 1961 visit to India.

12. Martin Luther King, Jr., Strength to Love 138 (1963).

13. *Id.* at 139.
14. James P. Hanigan, Martin Luther King, Jr., and the Foundations of Nonviolence 83 (1984).
15. *Id.* at 184.
16. Martin Luther King, Jr., A Knock at Midnight 110–111 (1998).
17. King, *supra* note 6 at 275.
18. *Id.* at 275.
19. King, *supra* note 16 at 58.
20. *Id.* at 49.
21. Keith D. Miller, Voice of Deliverance: The Language of Martin Luther King and its Sources 53 (1992).
22. *Id.* at 46.
23. King, *supra* note 16 at 96–97.
24. *Id.* at 55.
25. *Id.* at 57.
26. *Id.* at 97–98.
27. Martin Luther King, Jr., The Power of Non-Violence (June 4, 1957), http://www.teachingamericanhistory.org/library/index.asp?documentprint=1131.
28. Martin Luther King, Jr., Where Do We Go From Here: Chaos or Community 37 (1968).
29. *Id.* at 37.
30. 2 Thomas Aquinas, Quodlibet, Question 4, a. 1, 89 (1949).
31. Thomas Aquinas, Summa Contra Gentiles, III, Part II, 125–126 (1975).
32. *Id.* at Providence 161.
33. Thomas Aquinas, On Aristotle's Love and Friendship 82 (1951).
34. 2 Thomas Aquinas, Summa Theologica, English Dominican Friars, trans., II-II, Q. 34, a. 3, 1342 (1948).
35. *Id.* at II-II, Q. 23, a. 8, 1275.
36. *Id.*
37. Jason Lloyd, *Let There Be Justice: A Thomistic Assessment of Utilitarianism and Libertarianism*, 8 Tex. Rev. L. & Pol. 252 (2003).

38. J.V. Dolan, *Natural Law and Modern Jurisprudence*, LAVAL THEOLOGIQUE ET PHILOSOPHIQUE 44 (1990).

39. 1 THOMAS AQUINAS, SUMMA THEOLOGICA, English Dominican Friars, trans., I-II, Q. 93, a. 3, (1948).

40. Aquinas, *supra* note 31 at 124.

41. Aquinas, *supra* note 39 at I-II, Q. 91, a. 2, 997.

42. Iredell Jenkins, *The Concept of Rights and the Competence of Courts*, 18 AM. J. JURIS. 2 (1973).

43. KARL KREILKAMP, THE METAPHYSICAL FOUNDATIONS OF THOMISTIC JURISPRUDENCE 136 (1939).

44. King, *supra* note 12 at 74.

45. MARTIN LUTHER KING, JR., BOSTON UNIVERSITY COLLECTION XIV, 67.

46. King, *supra* note 12 at 86.

47. King, *supra* note 7 at 123; *See also* KEITH D. MILLER, VOICE OF DELIVERANCE: THE LANGUAGE OF MARTIN LUTHER KING, JR. 167 (1992).

48. *Id.* at 116.

49. *Id.* at 312.

50. MARTIN LUTHER KING, JR., THE MEASURE OF A MAN 49 (2001).

51. Aquinas, *supra* note 39 at I-II, Q. 93, a. 3, 1005.

52. THOMAS AQUINAS, AN APOLOGY FOR THE RELIGIOUS ORDERS 591 (1902).

53. *Id.* at 596.

54. Kirk A. Kennedy, *Reaffirming the Natural Law Jurisprudence of Justice Clarence Thomas*, 34 REGENT U. L. REV. 43 (1997).

55. King, *supra* note 12 at 113.

56. King, *supra* note 16 at 27.

57. MARTIN LUTHER KING, JR., I'VE BEEN TO THE MOUNTAINTOP 19 (1994).

58. King, *supra* note 16 at 27.

59. *Id.* at 27.

60. MCINERNY, ETHICA THOMISTICA: THE MORAL PHILOSOPHY OF THOMAS AQUINAS 30 (1982).

61. Aquinas, *supra* note 39 at I-II, Q. 5, a. 1, 609.

62. Aquinas, *supra* note 34 at II-II, Q. 40, 1359.

63. *Id.* at II-II, Q. 64, a. 7, 1471.

64. Hanigan, *supra* note 14 at 184.

65. King, *supra* note 28 at 26.

66. Thomas Aquinas, On Kingship: To the Ruler of Cyprus (1982).

67. King, *supra* note 28 at 44.

68. *Id.*

69. *Id.* at 188.

70. King, *supra* note 3 at 6.

71. King, *supra* note 28 at 59.

72. *Id.* at 62.

73. King, *supra* note 27.

74. *Id.*

75. King, *supra* note 28 at 191.

Chapter 4

1. 2 Thomas Aquinas, Summa Theologica, English Dominican Friars, trans., II-II, Q. 96, a 4, 1019 (1948).

2. Martin Luther King, Jr., Strength to Love 23 (1963).

3. Aquinas, *supra* note 1 at II-II, Q. 92, a. 1, 1002.

4. Martin Luther King, Jr., The Triumph of Conscience 48 (1967).

5. *Id.* at 8.

6. St. Thomas Aquinas, On Kingship: To the King of Cyprus, Gerard Phelan, trans., 12 (1982).

7. Aquinas, *supra* note 1 at II-II, Q. 104, a. 5, 1645.

8. James T. McHugh, *The Value of a Religiously Affiliated Law School*, 74 St. John's L. Rev. 587 (2000).

9. Aquinas, *supra* note 1 at II-II, Q. 104, a. 5, 1645.

10. Modern legal philosophers tend to dislike this form of black and white thinking. In other words, the question of obligation should not depend on some perennial truths such as those espoused in the natural law thinking of Aquinas. *See* R. George Wright, *Legal Obligation and the Law*, 23 Ga. L. Rev. 997 (1989).

11. Aquinas, *supra* note 6 at 18.

12. Thomas Aquinas, An Apology for the Religious Orders 599–600 (1902).

13. Aquinas, *supra* note 6 at 47.

14. Cicero, De Legibus, Clinton Keyes, trans., (1948).

15. Thomas Aquinas, Summa Contra Gentiles: Volume III: Providence 163 (1975).

16. Aquinas, *supra* note 6 at 12.

17. Aristotle, Nicomachean Ethics, Hippocrates G. Apostle, trans., (1984).

18. 1 Thomas Aquinas, Summa Theologica, English Dominican Friars, trans., I-II, Q. 90, a.2, 997 (1947).

19. John F. Coverdale, *The Legacy of John Paul II*, 36 Seton Hall L. Rev. 14 (2005).

20. *See generally*, Henry Mather, *Natural Law and Right Answers*, 38 Am. J. Juris. 297 (1993).

21. *See* Charles P. Nemeth, Aquinas in the Courtroom (2001); Robert P. George, *Natural Law and Human Nature, in* Natural Law Theory 34 (1992).

22. John Finnis, Natural Law and Natural Right 290 (1980).

23. *See* G. Edward White, *From Realism to Critical Legal Studies: A Truncated Intellectual History,* 40 Sw. L. J. 819 (1986).

24. Coverdale, *supra* note 19 at 36.

25. Aquinas, *supra* note 18 at I-II, Q. 95, a. 2.

26. *Id.* at I-II, Q. 93, a. 3, ad. 2.

27. Patrick M. J. Clancy, *St. Thomas on Law, in* 3 Thomas Aquinas, Summa Theologica 3270 (English Dominican Friars, trans., 1947).

28. Martin Luther King, Jr., Where Do We Go From Here: Chaos or Community 100 (1968).

29. Martin Luther King, Jr., A Knock at Midnight 28 (1998).

30. William H. Pryor, Jr., *Christian Duty and the Rule of Law,* 34 Cumberland L. Rev. 5 (2003).

31. Aquinas, *supra* note 6 at 24.

32. *Id.* at 26.

33. Aquinas, *supra* note 18 at I-II, Q. 94, 1008.

34. The tension between public office and corresponding duties was quite evidence in the Judge Moore case in Alabama which dealt with the removal of the Ten Commandments from the Courthouse. Those who might compare this duty to resist with that propounded by Aquinas miss the point. It is doubtful Aquinas would have ever called for resistance in this case because of the subject matter. *See* Pryor, *supra* note 30.

35. Charles E. Rice, *Some Reasons for a Restoration of Natural Law Jurisprudence*, 24 WAKE FOREST L. REV. 553 (1989).

36. Rufus Burrow, Jr., *Martin Luther King, Jr., and the Objective Moral Order: Some Ethical Implications*, 61 ENCOUNTER 221 (2000).

37. 2 MARTIN LUTHER KING, JR., THE PAPERS OF MARTIN LUTHER KING, JR., 252 (1994).

38. *Id.* at 252–253.

39. CICERO, DE LEGIBUS (1967).

40. King, *supra* note 2 at 105.

41. "I HAVE A DREAM," THE QUOTATIONS OF MARTIN LUTHER KING, JR. 79 (Lotte Hoskins, ed., 1968).

42. MARTIN LUTHER KING, JR., THE POWER OF NONVIOLENCE, (June 4, 1957), http://edsitement.neh.gov/lessonplans/mlking.html.

43. John J. Fitzgerald, *Today's Catholic Law Schools in Theory and Practice: Are We Preserving Our Identity?* NOTRE DAME L. J. ETHICS & PUB. POL'Y 270 (2001).

44. Aquinas, *supra* note 18 at I-II, Q. 94, art. 5, 1011.

45. Roger J. Kiley, *Human Law, in* 3 THOMAS AQUINAS, SUMMA THEOLOGICA 3275 (English Dominican Friars, trans., 1947).

46. Aquinas, *supra* note 18 at I-II, Q. 94, art. 3, 1010.

47. Mark Edward DeForrest, *Civil Disobedience: Its Nature and Role in the American Legal Landscape*, 13 GONZAGA L. REV. 661–662 (2004).

48. Aquinas, *supra* note 18 at I-II, Q. 94, art. 2, 1009.

49. *See* Thomas A. Fay, *The Development of St. Thomas's Teaching on the Distinction Between the Primary and Secondary Precepts of Natural Law*, 46 DOCTOR COMMUNIS 266 (1993).

50. R. A. ARMSTRONG, PRIMARY AND SECONDARY PRECEPTS IN THOMISTIC NATURAL LAW TEACHING 131 (1966).

51. Aquinas, *supra* note 18 at I-II, Q. 94, art. 4, 1009.

52. *Id.* at I-II, Q. 94, art. 5, 1011.

53. *Id.* at I-II, Q. 94, art. 6, 1012.

54. *Id.* at I-II, Q. 94, art. 6, 1013.

55. Martin Golding, *Aquinas and Some Contemporary Natural Law Theories*, 48 PROCEEDINGS OF THE AMERICAN CATHOLIC PHILOSOPHICAL ASSOCIATION 238 (1974).

56. Daniel A. Degnan, *Two Models of Positive Law in Aquinas: A Study of the Relationship of Positive and Natural Law*, THOMIST 5 (1982).

57. Aquinas, *supra* note 18 at I-II, Q. 95, art. 2, 1014.

Chapter 5

1. ALBERT C. KNUDSON, THE PHILOSOPHY OF PERSONALISM (1949).

2. MARTIN LUTHER KING, JR., STRENGTH TO LOVE 111 (1964).

3. Martin Luther King, Jr., *The Ethical Demands for Integration, in* A TESTAMENT OF HOPE, 119 (Washington, ed., 1986).

4. 1 THOMAS AQUINAS, SUMMA THEOLOGICA, English Dominican Friars, trans., I, Q. 2, a. 3, 13 (1948).

5. *Id.* at I, Q. 2, a. 3, 13.

6. MARTIN LUTHER KING, JR., LETTER FROM BIRMINGHAM JAIL 3 (April 16, 1963), http://www.stanford.edu/group/King/speeches.

7. Rufus Burrow, Jr., *Personalism, the Objective Moral Order, and Moral Law in the Work of Martin Luther King, Jr., in* THE LEGACY OF MARTIN LUTHER KING, JR., 213 (2002).

8. Barbara A. Holmes & Susan Holmes Winfied, *King, the Constitution and the Courts: Remaining Awake through the Great Revolution, in* THE LEGACY OF MARTIN LUTHER KING, JR., 193 (2002).

9. 2 THOMAS AQUINAS, SUMMA THEOLOGICA, English Dominican Friars, trans., II-III, Q. 96, a. 6, 1021(1948).

10. *Id.* at II-III, Q. 58, a. 3, 1436.

11. 1 THOMAS AQUINAS, SUMMA THEOLOGICA, English Dominican Friars, trans., I-II, Q. 93, a. 3, 1008 (1948).

12. King, *supra* note 6.

13. MARTIN LUTHER KING, JR., WHY WE CAN'T WAIT 85 (1964).

14. Holmes & Winfied, *supra* note 8 at 193.

15. JAMES P. HANIGAN, MARTIN LUTHER KING, JR., AND THE FOUNDATIONS OF NONVIOLENCE 101 (1984).

16. *Id.* at 83.

17. Aquinas, *supra* note 11 at I-II, Q. 93, a. 3, 1005.

18. *Id.* at I-II, Q. 93, a. 3, 1005.

19. ST. THOMAS AQUINAS, SUMMA CONTRA GENTILES: VOLUME III: PROVIDENCE 161 (1975).

20. MARTIN LUTHER KING, JR., BOSTON UNIVERSITY COLLECTION XIV, 67 http://www.bu.edu/mlkjr.

21. *Id.* at 32.

22. *Id.* at 27.

23. MARTIN LUTHER KING, JR., A KNOCK AT MIDNIGHT 27 (1998).

24. MARTIN LUTHER KING, JR., WHERE DO WE GO FROM HERE: CHAOS OR COMMUNITY 59 (1968).

25. Aquinas, *supra* note 11 at I-II, Q. 91, a. 2, 997.

26. *Id.* at I-II, Q. 96, a. 4, 1020.

27. Martin Luther King, Jr., *Is It All Right to Break the Law?* U.S. NEWS & WORLD REP., Aug. 12, 1963.

28. "I HAVE A DREAM": THE QUOTATIONS OF MARTIN LUTHER KING, JR. 139 (Lotte Hoskins, comp. & ed., 1968).

29. Aquinas, *supra* note 11 at I-II, Q. 93, a. 3, 1005.

Index